The Soviet Presence in Latin America

The Soviet Presence in Latin America

JAMES D. THEBERGE

PUBLISHED BY

Crane, Russak &
Company, Inc.
NEW YORK

National Strategy
Information Center, Inc.

The Soviet Presence in Latin America

Published in the United States by
Crane, Russak & Company, Inc.
347 Madison Avenue
New York, N.Y. 10017

Library Edition: ISBN 0-8448-0357-X

Paperbound Edition: ISBN 0-8448-0514-9

LC 74-82929

Strategy Paper No. 23

Printed in the United States of America

Table of Contents

Preface

Russian involvement in Latin American affairs is a relatively recent development. Tsarist foreign policy paid little attention to this geographically remote corner of the globe. After 1917, Russia's new Communist masters sought to promote revolution wherever possible. But even for them, Latin America was not a high priority target. Much more promising revolutionary opportunities beckoned in other areas. To be sure, the Kremlin did work hard to create loyal, disciplined Communist parties throughout the region. But only since the end of World War II has Latin America become a major target of Soviet ambition.

In the present monograph, Mr. James D. Theberge analyzes the evolution of Soviet policy toward Latin America in the postwar period. He gives special attention to the main instruments of Kremlin policy: traditional diplomacy (supported in recent years by a growing Soviet naval presence in the Caribbean), trade and aid, espionage and subversion, and selective support for revolutionary violence. A chapter is devoted to the Kremlin's relations with the various Communist and other revolutionary parties of Latin America. Moscow's dealings with Fidel Castro's Cuba, as well as with the now-defunct Allende government in Chile and the still-incumbent revolutionary military regime in Peru, are also examined in detail.

Mr. Theberge points out that Moscow's present objectives in Latin America are still severely limited: "to strengthen Soviet influence wherever possible, to defend 'Socialist' Cuba, and to weaken the still predominant position of the United States." It is a cautious policy, "designed to extend Soviet influence without risking a military confrontation." The Soviets apparently recognize that they cannot hope to establish political predominance in the region in the foreseeable future.

On the other hand, Moscow's long-term ambitions are also perfectly clear — namely, the achievement of political power wherever possible. It is the author's judgment that the Soviet position in Latin America is "stronger today than it was a decade ago," although still "far from a commanding position;" and it is getting stronger. Moreover, the Russians seem likely to continue this gradual effort to shift the balance of power. "Despite detente, Moscow shows no signs of abandoning its policy of taking advantage of any change in Latin America that can be used against the United States." The ultimate implications of this steady erosion of the US position must give serious concern to Washington policymakers in the years ahead.

Mr. Theberge is at the Center for Strategic and International Studies at Georgetown University. He has written and lectured extensively on Latin American political and economic problems. He received his B.A. at Columbia University, his M.A. at Oxford University, and his M.P.A. at Harvard University. Among his other published books is *Russia in the Caribbean*. He was also a contributing editor to *Soviet Seapower in the Caribbean, Political and Strategic Implications,* and a contributing author to *The Stability of the Caribbean*. He was a Littauer Fellow at Harvard University, 1964-65, a Special Advisor to the Secretary of the Treasury in 1966, and a Federal German Republic Fellow at Heidelberg University in 1957-58.

Frank R. Barnett, *President*
National Strategy Information Center, Inc.

June 1974

1

Russian Interest in Latin America

Russia has had very little interest in Latin America until recent times. Tsarist Russia had only the most sporadic and tenuous contacts with the Spanish-American colonies in the 18th century and the newly independent Latin American republics in the 19th century.[1] Russian trading outposts, pushing south from Alaska along the Pacific coast, alarmed the Spanish Viceroy of Mexico and, after independence, the new rulers of Mexico, who feared Russian designs on the fertile provinces of upper and lower California.[2] But aside from this southward encroachment and the dispatch of an occasional scientific expedition to the region, Russia's relations with Latin America were virtually nonexistent until the latter half of the 19th century.[3] Diplomatic and commercial ties were

[1] Feodor Karzhavin, a writer and translator, was the first Russian to spend some time in Latin America. He visited Cuba in 1782-84. Francisco Miranda, a leader of the Latin American independence movement, traveled to Russia and became a favorite of Catherine the Great. See Victor Vol'skii, "The Study of Latin America in the U.S.S.R.," in J. Gregory Oswald, *Soviet Image of Contemporary Latin America, A Documentary History 1960-1968* (Austin: University of Texas Press, 1970), p. 13.

[2] See Stephen Clissold, ed., *Soviet Relations with Latin America, 1918-1968, A Documentary Survey* (London: Oxford University Press, 1970), p. 1.

[3] During the 19th century, Russia did maintain relations with Brazil, which was not, however, an independent republic but a monarchy ruled by a branch of the Portuguese Bragança dynasty.

established with Argentina in 1885, Mexico in 1887, and Uruguay in 1890. Latin America was too remote from the Russian homeland, had no strategic importance, and altogether too little to offer to engage the serious attention of Tsarist statesmen.

After the 1917 revolution, Tsarist foreign policy patterns were replaced by the farreaching messianic ambitions of the Bolsheviks. To be sure, Latin America did not figure prominently among them because, as Lenin declared, far more urgent revolutionary tasks faced the new Soviet leadership.[4] Moreover, the strength of "American imperialism" in the region and the rudimentary state of the Socialist movement did not favor Communist revolution. Latin America was not entirely neglected; but Moscow was more interested in using Latin America to influence British and American policies elsewhere than in making revolution on the scene.

The founding of local Communist parties and the Latin American section of the Comintern, and the opening of diplomatic relations with Mexico in August 1924, created fresh opportunities for promoting Soviet interests.[5] Under Comintern guidance, the Mexican Communist Party was far more successful in fostering communism in Central America than in Mexico itself, where the Mexican people clearly preferred to make their own revolution without Soviet assistance. Farther south, Soviet influence scored some gains in the Rio de la Plata countries, and especially in Argentina, whose Communist Party was the first in Latin America to join the Comintern. A South American Comintern secretariat was set up in Buenos Aires in 1930 and given the task of strengthening Soviet influence and supervising the flow of agents in the southern zones of the continent.[6]

[4]M.N. Roy, *Memoirs* (Bombay: 1964), p. 346.

[5]Mexico was the first Latin American nation to establish diplomatic relations with the USSR. Uruguay followed suit two years later in 1926.

[6]Soviet-Latin American relations in the interwar period are discussed in detail by Stephen Clissold, "Soviet Relations with Latin America between the Wars," in J. Gregory Oswald and Anthony J. Stover, eds., *The Soviet Union and Latin America* (New York; Praeger, 1970), pp. 15-23.

Between the two World Wars, Moscow's policy aimed at creating loyal, disciplined local Communist parties, enhancing Soviet influence through normal diplomatic and trade channels, and eroding the predominant British and American position. This policy faced, however, the now-familiar dilemma of attempting to reconcile the foreign policy interests of Moscow with the needs of local parties and the narrow, sectarian approach of the Comintern. In the later 1920s and the 1930s, the meddling, ultraleftist tactics of the Comintern not only made little progress but provoked a rupture of diplomatic relations with Mexico (1930), Argentina (1930), Chile (1932), Brazil (1936), and Uruguay (1936). But it is doubtful whether Russia would have made much more headway even if Soviet policy had been more flexible and Comintern tactics less extreme. A revolutionary situation did not exist in Latin America. Despite some popular unrest, the traditional Latin American elites and their military allies were still firmly in the saddle.

The rise of popular parties, European immigration that brought radical social ideas, the emergence of militant labor organizations and a reformist middle class leadership, and the large influx of rural poor to the cities created conditions of political and social unrest in Latin America during the first two decades after the Russian revolution. But the Soviet Union was in no position to take advantage of a situation that seemed propitious for the appearance of radical political groups and the spread of Marxist ideas. Moscow's ignorance of the region, its contemptuous attitude toward Latin American culture and traditions, and the dogmatic inflexibility of Comintern directives to local Communist parties did not help matters. But the main problem was that the Soviet Union was deeply absorbed in its own domestic problems, and Latin America simply did not figure high on the list of Soviet priorities. In the 1930s, moreover, radical Latin American nationalists riding the wave of the future were far more inclined to opt for German Nazism or Italian fascism than for Russian communism.

Some progress was made in creating loyal and disciplined local Communist parties, and a few of them enjoyed a measure of electoral success. In Chile, the organization of a strong Communist Party contributed to formation of a popular front coalition which brought the Radical Party and its presidential candidate, Pedro Aquirre Cerda, to power in 1938. Thus, Chile became the third country (after France and Spain) to be ruled by popular fronts, thereby demonstrating the viability of the Comintern strategy even in remote areas. Despite the meager results in the interwar period, the groundwork was laid for the expansion of propaganda work, and valuable experience gained in Latin American politics and society.

TABLE 1

Founding of Latin American Communist Parties

Country	*Year*
Argentina	1918
Mexico	1919
Uruguay	1920
Chile	1922
Brazil	1922
Cuba	1925
Honduras	1927
Ecuador	1928
Guatemala	1931
Venezuela	1931
Puerto Rico	1932
Paraguay	1933
Nicaragua	1939
Guadeloupe	1944
Martinique	1944
Dominican Republic	1944
Bolivia	1950
Haiti	1959

Source: G. N. Kolomiets, ed., *Politicheskie partii stran Latinskoi Ameriki* (Moscow: Institut Latinskoi Ameriki Akademii Nauk SSSR, 1955).

For a brief period during and immediately after World War II
(1941-47), Soviet Russia and the local Communist parties acquired
considerable influence. The wartime alliance between the USSR
and the Western powers improved the political climate and facilitated the expansion of Soviet diplomatic contacts with Latin
America.[7] Local Communist parties were directed by Moscow to
support the Allied war effort and to use their influence to prevent
strikes and the disruption of war production. But the onset of the
Cold War in 1947 soon reversed this trend. Soviet relations with
Latin America became increasingly strained as Stalin bitterly
criticized the Latin American governments, especially their close
ties with the United States, and demanded that the local parties
publicly declare their loyalty to the Soviet Union. Wartime
goodwill toward the USSR dissipated quickly, diplomatic relations
were severed, and the Communist parties outlawed.

The rigidity of Stalinist policy and the intransigence of local
Communist parties at the height of the Cold War made it all but
impossible for Russia to collaborate with the Latin American
countries during this period. Stalin appeared convinced that there
was no middle ground between the Soviet bloc and the capitalist
camp headed by the United States. There were a few signs of a shift
away from this inflexible position even before Stalin's death. But it
was only after 1953 that a basic policy reorientation became evident, and Russia once more began to establish diplomatic,
commercial, and cultural ties with the Latin American countries.

Present Soviet Aims

Moscow's present objectives in Latin America are easily defined: to strengthen Soviet influence wherever possible, to defend
"Socialist" Cuba, and to weaken the still predominant position of
the United States. To these ends, the Soviet Union has been
prepared to cooperate with democrats, dictators, and ultraradical
revolutionaries, even when they are militantly anti-Communist.

---

[7]In 1939, Moscow had no diplomatic ties with any Latin American country. By
1946, it had relations with 13 countries, and the Latin American Communist
parties achieved a new high point of influence and prestige.

Moscow showed great patience in the face of Castro's early defiance, and turned a blind eye to the suppression of communism in Brazil and Argentina. An anti-Communist government pursuing a foreign policy friendly to the Soviet Union is now preferred to a Socialist state that resists Soviet influence; an amenable yet basically anti-Communist regime, like Velasco's military dictatorship in Peru, appears to suit current Soviet purposes better than Tito's Yugoslavia.

Since the 1962 missile crisis, Khrushchev's adventurism in Latin America has been replaced by a more cautious policy designed to extend Soviet influence without risking a military confrontation with the United States. A wide range of well-orchestrated policy instruments is employed by Moscow: diplomacy, propaganda, espionage, political agitation, revolutionary violence, military and economic aid, and even naval power. The Soviet Union now combines a more active "traditional" diplomacy that seeks normal state-to-state relations with bourgeois governments, with a massive build-up of strategic military forces and a growing naval presence to support its diplomacy. It has also intensified its "ideological-missionary" guidance to local Communist parties and front groups and its covert support of revolutionary violence.

Ideological Formulations

The Soviet Union looks upon Latin America as occupying a special position in the Third World. It is an area of relatively mature capitalism where, however, the necessary "objective" and "subjective" conditions for a Communist victory are lacking. Armed struggle is opposed not as a matter of principle, but only because of the poor prospects for success and the adverse effects that premature attempts to seize power would have on Russian national interests. Latin America's backwardness requires a "transitional stage" to prepare the political and economic base for Socialist reconstruction. Moscow believes that the region must first pass through a "popular democratic" revolutionary phase on the path to socialism.

While Soviet perceptions of Latin America are ideologically weighed down by Marxist class analysis, studies of individual countries show increasing sophistication. Most categorizations in Soviet literature refer to Latin America as a whole; but increasingly, the Caribbean region is perceived to have special characteristics that set it apart. It is viewed by Moscow as the most sensitive zone in the "strategic rear" of the United States, and the only region of Latin America where the United States has recently intervened with military force. It is also recognized as retaining especially close political, military, and economic ties with the United States.

In current Soviet Latin American strategy, the local Communist parties are urged to play a prominent role in left-wing coalitions, radical revolutionary governments, even "progressive" military regimes. The strategy requires Communist participation in popular front alliances and coalitions, penetration of the "progressive" segments of the national bourgeoisie, and the mobilization and radicalization of the masses. In an era of East-West detente, it also requires that Soviet support for Latin American revolutionary movements be given in such a way as not to endanger improved relations with the United States.

Moscow harbors no illusion that "peaceful" accession to power by pro-Soviet Communist or Marxist-oriented parties through united front tactics will be easy or that it can be achieved without intense class conflict and violence. The dramatic overthrow of Chile's Socialist-Communist coalition in September 1973 made abundantly clear that the "peaceful path" is beset with difficulties. As a result of the Chilean experience, Latin American military and democratic political leaders are more aware of Soviet and Cuban intervention than before. The fact that the Communist movement in Latin America is severely splintered and that the "unity of left-wing and democratic forces" is still far more a slogan than a reality, compounds the problems on the "peaceful path" to socialism.

For a time after the Allende victory in Chile, it appeared that the peaceful, electoral route to socialism might be successful elsewhere in the region. But the Russians showed considerable caution in their support of Allende and skepticism about the prospects for a successful Communist seizure of power. The defeat of the candidate of the leftist coalition (*Frente Amplia*) in Uruguay in the November 1971 presidential election, the military coup in Chile in September 1973, and the small vote obtained by the left-wing coalition (*Nueva Fuerza*) in Venezuela's December 1973 presidential election, have shown that the electoral path faces formidable obstacles in Latin America.

At present, Moscow does not foresee an early victory for communism in any Latin American country. It now favors a long period of transition from coalition governments to communism, in order to restrict its political and economic commitments to what it can afford. A successful revolution would obligate the Soviet Union to insure the survival of the new Communist regime and this would severely limit Soviet options. Moscow would like to see these countries achieve self-sustaining levels of capital accumulation and development prior to Communist takeover so that the new Communist regimes would have a better chance of survival and not make embarrassing demands on the USSR. This was evident in the case of Chile under Allende. After the costly Cuban entanglement, the Soviet Union encouraged Allende to obtain capital from the capitalist states, to pursue a policy of self-help and not to expect large-scale Soviet aid.

Legal and Revolutionary Methods of Struggle

While the Soviet Union and Moscow-oriented Communist parties in Latin America emphasize "constitutional" or "legal" methods of struggle, Moscow's policy is essentially opportunistic and embraces all forms of struggle, peaceful or violent, legal or illegal, singly or in combination, depending on the opportunities offered by local political conditions. The local pro-Soviet parties are advised that they must always be prepared to "meet any eventuality" (including armed struggle) if power cannot be achieved peacefully.

The Soviet Union advocates "peaceful" methods of struggle (which, however, do not exclude class conflict and even violence) whenever they promise success or gain, and condemns armed struggle as "revolutionary adventurism" when failure seems likely. In countries like Guatemala and Nicaragua, where the "peaceful path" to socialism is blocked, Moscow is prepared to consider revolutionary violence as a possible vehicle of change. But elaborate precautions are taken to conceal Soviet sponsorship of internal subversion and revolutionary violence. Whenever possible, Moscow employs Cuban and East European proxies to conduct high-risk operations that would embarrass the USSR in case of failure. This can be done because the Soviet Union so completely dominates the intelligence services of Cuba, Czechoslovakia, East Germany, Poland, Hungary, and to some extent Rumania, that for all practical purposes they are mere extensions of Soviet intelligence.[8]

Moscow has both opportunities and problems in extending its influence into Latin America. The powerful economic and cultural impact of the United States on the Latin American countries works in Moscow's favor. It has turned the United States into the primary target of local nationalists striving for independent development and a scapegoat for their intractable problems. The upsurge of economic nationalism, restrictions on the operations of multinational corporations, the emergence of left-wing military dictatorships, the strong populist trend in many countries, and the temporary success of the united front strategy in Chile in 1970, also seemed to be working in Moscow's favor. Moscow views these developments as having weakened Washington's political and economic predominance in Latin America and opened up new opportunities for ideological penetration at minimum risk and cost.

In current Soviet strategy, considerable tactical stress is given to taking advantage of middle class nationalism in order to

---

[8]See John Barron, *KGB* (New York: Reader's Digest Press, 1974), p. 22; and Orlando Castro Hidalgo, *Spy for Fidel* (Miami: Seemann Publishing, 1971), pp. 62-63.

strengthen local Communist movements and foster closer relations with Moscow. The Soviets hope to intensify and exploit the anti-imperialist potential of the "national bourgeoisie" (that is, supporters of the liberal market economy) who feel threatened by the intrusion of foreign capital and favor diplomatic and trade relations with the Communist bloc as a counterweight to American influence. The national bourgeoisie is expected gradually to lose faith in foreign investment as a vehicle of technological progress, industrial development, and higher living standards. Anti-American, anti-foreign capital elements within the Latin American military, bureaucratic, technical, and intellectual elites are considered to be especially responsive to Communist "anti-imperialist" propaganda, and are marked down as potential allies.

Nationalist sectors of the middle class are viewed as the decisive force behind the "national liberation" movements in Latin America and the Caribbean. Moscow believes that a coalition of Communist, left-wing, and middle class nationalist forces — united by their hostility to growing US economic power and frustrated at the pace of social progress — will eventually gain power in peaceful political competition, or acquire decisive influence through cooperation with "progressive" military regimes. These regimes, whether civilian or military, will then seek Soviet support in their struggle for independence from the United States.

The Soviet presence in Latin America in the 1970s is much more visible than a decade ago. Moscow has made a heavy investment in Cuba, and staked its prestige on the survival of the Castro regime. The Russians also have acquired considerable influence in Peru under the Velasco regime, and in Chile under Allende; and the "populist" Peron government in Argentina and the military dictatorship in Panama also seem to offer possibilities.

But Soviet policy has also encountered serious difficulties. The continued weakness of Cuba under Castro is not a good advertisement for the efficiency of communism. So long as Moscow was not heavily involved in Latin American affairs, it enjoyed a certain prestige precisely because of its apparent role as a remote onlooker without specific interests or responsibilities in the area. But as the Russians became more involved in Latin American politics, the aura of disinterested altruism began to disappear. Nationalist mistrust of the USSR is already considerable, and can be expected to grow. Latin American nationalists are quite willing to use the Soviet Union against the United States, but they are anxious to avoid Cuba's mistake of replacing dependence on America with subservience to the Soviet Union. Moreover, the establishment of client states involves certain costs and risks. Once enmeshed in such relationships, it is difficult to get out of obligations and cut losses. Having provided large-scale military and economic assistance to Cuba for over a decade, Moscow could not now readily discontinue its support, however costly the venture and unpromising the long-term prospects. The military coup in Chile was interpreted as a Soviet defeat, and Moscow's reluctance to come to the aid of the Allende regime was seen as an admission of weakness.

As for the future, the Soviet Union will continue attempts to strengthen its position in the Hemisphere and to consolidate its hold on Cuba. But various factors tend to restrain the Soviet Union from adopting a more adventurous policy. Among them are the risks and uncertainties of the possible American reaction, and the effect that a forward policy would have on Soviet-American relations. Moscow must also consider the possible material costs that further economic and military commitments in the region might entail, and the vulnerability of any Soviet military position in the Hemisphere.

2

Soviet Diplomacy

Prior to the 1960s, Moscow's political and economic relations with Latin America were marginal at best, and efforts to broaden relations with the countries of the region often ended in frustration. At the time of Stalin's death in 1953, for example, Russia had formal diplomatic relations with only three of them (Argentina, Mexico, and Uruguay).[9]

During the optimistic Khrushchev years, when Moscow showed greater interest in courting the Third World, some attention was given to establishing diplomatic and commercial ties with the Latin American countries.[10] Latin America remained a low priority, however, until after Castro seized power in Cuba and adopted Marxism-Leninism as a guide to national development. Moscow's expanding military, economic, and technological capabilities also made it possible for the Soviet Union to pursue a

[9]See Clissold, op. cit., pp. 1-59; and J. Gregory Oswald, "Soviet Diplomatic Relations with Mexico, Uruguay and Cuba," in Donald Herman, ed., The Communist Tide in Latin America (Austin: University of Texas Press, 1972), pp. 75-115.

[10]W. Raymond Duncan, "Soviet Policy in Latin America Since Khrushchev," Orbis, vol. 15, no. 2 (Summer 1971), pp. 643-669.

more active Latin American policy at this time. Conversely, the lessening of East-West tensions, the emergence of a leftist trend in several Latin American countries, the indigenous drive to industrialize and find new export markets, the persistence of nationalist hostility to the United States and the desire for greater independence from Washington, all served to stimulate interest on the part of an increasing number of Latin American countries in the resumption of diplomatic and commercial relations with the Soviet Union and the Socialist camp in general. Castro's Cuba was the first to reestablish full diplomatic relations with the Soviet Union in 1960; Brazil followed suit in 1961, and Chile in 1964.[11] Colombia followed in 1968; Peru, Bolivia, and Ecuador in 1969; Venezuela and Guyana in 1970; and Costa Rica in 1971. By 1970, the Soviets had diplomatic ties with all the South American countries except Paraguay; its diplomatic offensive in the Caribbean was somewhat less successful.[12]

By expanding its diplomatic, economic, scientific, and technical ties, the Soviet Union apparently hopes to wean the Latin American countries away from close relations with the United States, and to encourage a more neutral foreign policy orientation. To these ends, Moscow encourages Latin American participation in the conferences of the nonaligned nations (such as the Algiers conference of September 1973), the coordination of Latin American and Afro-Asian policy with respect to commodity export prices, restrictions on the activities of multinational corporations, the nationalization of foreign business holdings, and the adoption of anticolonial positions *vis-à-vis* Panama and Puerto Rico in various international organizations.

Moscow's diplomatic effort has been accompanied by an increase in trade and aid flows to Latin America. The normalization of diplomatic relations has sometimes preceded the quicken-

[11]The Soviet Union severed relations with Chile in September 1973 as a gesture of disapproval of the military junta that overthrew the Allende regime.

[12]By the end of 1973, Moscow still had no diplomatic or consular relations with Barbados, the Dominican Republic, Guatemala, Haiti, Honduras, Jamaica, Nicaragua, Panama, or Trinidad.

ing of economic intercourse. At other times, as in the recent case of Costa Rica, the opposite is true. Moscow's purchase of surplus Costa Rican coffee opened the way to diplomatic relations between the two countries. The Soviets have skillfully suggested that trade with them opens a vast new export market for Latin American goods, and thus reduces their economic dependence on the United States. Nevertheless, the levels of trade and aid have been quite small, compared to Soviet efforts in other regions such as the Middle East and Asia.

Relaxation of East-West tensions in the early 1970s strongly affected the foreign policy orientation of many Latin American states. It undermined the Cold War rationale for keeping the Soviet Union, Cuba, and the People's Republic of China at arm's length, and promised tangible political and economic rewards for a more accommodating posture. Most Latin American countries are now coming to view the Soviet Union and other Communist states less as a "Communist menace" and more as potentially valuable trading partners and sources of much-needed capital and technology. To the Peruvian military regime, for example, the continuing economic and social backwardness of their country is judged a far greater threat to national security than Soviet subversion. Moreover, many aspects of Soviet aid policy are positively attractive to the Latin American countries: the aversion to direct investment, the unqualified recognition of local sovereignty over natural resources, and a willingness to trade technology for raw materials. In addition, the opening of diplomatic and trade relations with the Soviet Union and Cuba, especially if accompanied by "anti-imperialist" rhetoric, often serves to pacify the radical left at home.

In Latin America, the establishment of relations with the Communist bloc was once advertised as a gesture of national sovereignty and independence from Washington that aroused much popular support and improved a country's bargaining position *vis-à-vis* the United States. In the early 1960s, for example, the anti-Communist regimes of Rafael Trujillo in the Dominican Republic and "Papa Doc" Duvalier in Haiti threatened to turn to the Soviet Union if more favorable treatment from the United States was not forthcoming. In the Nixon-Kissinger era of improved East-West relations, of course, such a threat lacks much efficacy. US policy no longer opposes Soviet political and economic ties with the Latin American countries. In any event, once a country has recognized the Communist states, the political value of this "gesture of independence" is soon exhausted.

In the 1960s, Moscow's diplomatic and economic ties with such anti-Communist countries as Colombia and Brazil imposed obvious strains on its "special" relationship with Cuba. By the end of the decade, the situation had changed completely. Castro himself switched tactics for breaking out of Cuba's isolation, and gave up immediate hopes of igniting pro-Castro revolutions in Latin America. Havana showed a new willingness to normalize relations — initially with "progressive" regimes (such as Allende's Chile and Velasco's Peru) showing independence from the United States, but eventually even with such anti-Communist Caribbean states as Jamaica and Barbados. Increased Soviet economic leverage in Havana and the obvious failure of guerrilla strategy in Latin America persuaded Castro to postpone the continental revolution, and to align Cuba more closely with Moscow's policy of peaceful coexistence and the relaxation of tensions with capitalist states.

A growing number of OAS members have now recognized Cuba or expressed an interest in doing so. Chile's Marxist government recognized Cuba in November 1970, immediately after gaining power, and President Allende urged other Latin American countries to ignore the OAS sanction. In July 1972, Peru also recognized Cuba; and in December 1972, four English-speaking Caribbean states — Barbados, Guyana, Jamaica, and Trinidad —announced the resumption of diplomatic ties with the Castro regime. Argentina followed suit in May 1973. Panama, Ecuador, Venezuela, and Cost Rica have expressed varying degrees of interest in reestablishing relations; and Brazil is also reassessing its policy toward Cuba. But the momentum for recognizing Castro was temporarily weakened at the end of 1973 when Chile's military junta broke relations with Havana in September as a result of Cuban intervention in Chile's internal affairs during the Allende period.

Many Spanish-speaking Caribbean countries, much nearer to Cuba and more exposed to Castro-supported subversion, continue to support the OAS blockade. As long as Castro persists in interfering in their internal affairs, these countries feel that there should be no abandonment, unilaterally or multilaterally, of the policy of diplomatic and economic isolation. They demand that Castro end even his present attenuated policy of intervention as an essential condition to Cuba's readmission into the OAS. For his part, Castro has declared many times that Cuba would not rejoin the OAS under any circumstances. A move by Washington and Havana to normalize relations, which is not entirely out of the question over the next few years, would obviously bring Cuba's political and economic isolation to an effective end. It could also set in motion the process of Havana's gradual reintegration into the existing or a modified hemispheric system.

There is considerable awareness in Latin America that Soviet, Cuban, and East European embassies continue to engage in subversive activities even in the era of peaceful coexistence. The excessively large staffs assigned to Soviet and Communist bloc missions, and the long history of Communist "diplomats" meddling in the internal affairs of Latin American countries, have led to frequent public outcries and sharp government reactions, including the expulsion of the diplomats concerned. But Russia's recent diplomatic and commercial advances show that Moscow is much less feared than before. The political and economic benefits of relations with the Communist countries are now generally perceived to outweigh the costs and risks involved.

3

Soviet Trade and Aid

Since World War II, Soviet foreign trade has grown significantly, but has been largely confined to the Socialist bloc. Trade with Latin America, aside from Cuba, is still insignificant. Indeed, Latin America is the least important trading area of the Soviet Union, and trails far behind the Middle East, Africa, and Asia in this respect. Soviet trade with Latin America declined slightly from $186 million in 1966 to $126 million in 1972. Argentina and Brazil account for over two thirds of the total trade. Moscow's economic aid to the Velasco government in Peru will be reflected in an increasing volume of trade with that country in the 1970s. Except for Cuba, which runs a chronic deficit averaging about $300 million annually in recent years, the Latin American countries enjoy a trade surplus with the Soviet Union.

The irregular pattern of Soviet-Latin American trade reflects the heavy component of political opportunism in Moscow's trade relations with the region. Moscow often buys a particular export commodity in times of surplus (for example, coffee or sugar) on a one-time basis in order to reap such political gains as diplomatic recognition. Not all Soviet trade is politically motivated, of course.

The USSR also buys goods it needs, such as sugar from Brazil, and sells to pay for what it buys. Nevertheless, many important transactions can only be explained by noneconomic considerations, especially the trade flows generated by economic aid programs.

The low level of trade with Latin America is also due to the fact that, in general, the USSR has little need for many of the raw materials and foodstuffs exported by the Latin American countries. In fact, the USSR is an exporter of many of the same commodities, or has more accessible and cheaper sources of supply. Moreover, the record disproves Moscow's protestations that centrally planned economies provide for more stable trade than the gyrations of the free market. Soviet trade with Latin America is characterized by much wider fluctuations in trading volume than Western trade with the region. The only exception is Moscow's Cuban client.

It is widely believed that Soviet trade and aid are attractive in the Third World because of the generous financial terms offered (low interest rates and long amortization periods) and the possibility of repayment in locally produced goods. These repayment concessions are welcomed because they presumably ease the balance of payments problems of developing countries. The Latin American countries are beginning to discover, however, that economic relations with the Soviet Union incur costs as well as benefits. While repayment in local commodities is superficially attractive, it also reduces the supplies available for sales to Western countries, and thus earnings in convertible currencies. The benefits derived from the relatively soft terms of Soviet aid credits are also significantly reduced by the fact that they are tied to the purchase of inferior or unsuitable Soviet goods. In addition, price discrimination (Moscow often overvalues its aid deliveries, for example, and undervalues goods delivered in repayment) sharply reduces the economic value of Soviet aid to Latin America. Most Western aid is similarly tied, but does not usually suffer from these disadvantages.

Between 1958 and 1965, the developing countries paid an

TABLE 2

Soviet Trade with Latin America (excluding Cuba), 1960-72

(*in millions of US dollars*)

	1960	1961	1962	1963	1964	1965	1966	1967	1968	1969	1970	1971	1972
Turnover[a]	76	66	110	101	84	167	186	80	98	124	87	124	126
Exports	42	32	41	41	31	51	58	27	27	35	13	19	22
Imports	34	34	69	60	53	116	128	53	71	89	74	105	104
Balance[b]	+8	−2	−28	−19	−22	−65	−70	−26	−44	−54	−61	−86	−82
Latin American Share of Soviet Trade	0.7%	0.6%	0.8%	0.7%	0.5%	1.0%	1.1%	0.4%	0.5%	0.6%	0.4%	0.5%	0.6%

Source: Based on official statistics compiled by the International Trade Analysis Staff, US Department of Commerce.

[a]Soviet exports plus imports.
[b]Soviet exports minus imports. Soviet deficit (−), surplus (+).

average of 15 to 25 percent more for commodities purchased from
the Soviet Union than Western industrial countries paid for the
same commodities. Moreover, the Soviet Union paid an average of
10 to 15 percent less for imports from the developing countries
under its bilateral trade arrangements than it would have paid on
the world market.[13] The Soviet Union, in fact, strikes the kind of
hard "capitalist" bargain with its aid recipients and trading
partners that it so severely criticizes the West for. Typically, its
convertible hard currency reserves are not freely available to its
friends—as Fidel Castro and Salvador Allende found out to their
regret—in order to finance emergency import requirements such
as food, spare parts, and machinery from Western sources.

Moscow's trade and aid practices dispel the notion that the
Soviet Union has introduced a new and more progressive form of
international relations in its dealings with the Socialist states or
between the Soviet Union and the Third World. Within the
Communist world (including Cuba), the Soviet Union has acted as a
typical dominant power toward weaker states within its sphere of
influence. In recent years, Cuba has been pressured to reorient its
domestic and foreign policies, and to embrace peaceful coexistence
with the capitalist states under threat of the loss of Soviet aid.
Much greater restraint is necessarily shown in economic relations
with the developing countries of the non-Communist world. Still,
Moscow's trade and aid often come with political strings attached,
or result in inducements or pressures to make concessions to the
Soviet Union. Algeria, Indonesia, Ghana, Finland, and Iraq, for
example, are aid recipients that have been either penalized or
threatened for following policies of which Moscow disapproved.[14]
Economic agreements serve as a convenient means of establishing
Soviet trade and technical aid missions, negotiating cultural and
scientific cooperation agreements, training students, and placing
technicians and agents in strategic areas for the purpose of political

[13]James R. Carter, *The Net Cost of Soviet Foreign Aid* (New York: Praeger, 1971),
   pp. 39-41.
[14]Marshall Goldman, *Soviet Foreign Aid* (New York: Praeger, 1971), p. 196.

infiltration.[15] Technical aid missions, as in the case of Soviet technicians assigned to Chile's copper industry (whose services were paid for in dollars by the Allende government), are also used for industrial espionage.[16]

Cuba is the major Latin American trading partner of the Soviet Union, and the largest recipient by far of Soviet economic assistance. From 1960 to 1973, Soviet economic aid to Cuba, including balance of payments credits, technical assistance costs, project credits, and sugar subsidies, amounted to a cumulative total of about $5 billion. Soviet military aid amounts to another $2 billion, bringing total Soviet economic and military aid to an estimated $7 billion by the end of 1973.

The Soviet Union is particularly concerned about mounting Cuban trade indebtedness, which came to $2.3 billion in 1972. Cuba's trade debt, for which repayment prospects are not good, is expected to increase rapidly in the 1970s as a result of the sharp rise in the cost of Soviet crude oil shipments to Cuba. Prior to the dramatic hike in world oil prices, Moscow was providing about $100 million a year (in 1972) in crude oil to Cuba; but the value of oil shipments could rise to about $700 million in 1975, and over $1 billion in 1980. Moscow is understandably interested in minimizing oil shipments to Cuba (making Soviet oil available for hard currency sales on the world market), and in encouraging the resumption of Cuban oil imports from Venezuela, financed by foreign exchange earnings derived from trade with the United States and other Western countries.

From 1954 to 1972, Moscow made aid commitments of $8.3 billion (credits and grants) to the developing countries, but only $548 million (or 6.6 percent of the total) was for Latin America. About half of this amount went to Brazil and Chile; and in the

---

[15]US Department of State, Bureau of Intelligence and Research, *Research Memorandum* (September 18, 1972).

[16]According to a statement made to the author by Andres Zauschquevich, Executive Vice President of the Chilean Copper Corporation (CODELCO), in December 1973.

TABLE 3

Soviet Trade with Cuba, 1960-72

(in millions of US dollars)[a]

	1960	1961	1962	1963	1964	1965	1966	1967	1968	1969	1970	1971	1972
Turnover[b]	176.6	592.9	594.8	558.6	647.4	710.5	758.1	926.4	893.0	847.1	1149.5	802.6	679.1
Exports	73.9	284.1	363.1	395.8	362.3	371.7	475.1	557.4	618.0	617.8	638.0	542.3	509.3
Imports	102.7	308.8	231.7	162.8	285.1	338.8	283.0	369.0	275.0	229.3	511.5	260.3	169.8
Balance[c]	−28.8	−24.7	+131.4	+233.0	+77.2	+32.9	+192.1	+188.4	+343.0	+388.5	+126.5	+282.0	+339.5
Cuba's Share of Soviet Trade	1.6%	5.1%	4.5%	3.9%	4.2%	4.4%	4.5%	5.1%	4.5%	3.9%	4.7%	3.1%	3.2%

Source: U.S.S.R. Foreign Trade: Statistical Handbook, 1918-1966, and subsequent foreign trade annuals.

[a]Through 1971, converted to dollars at the rate of one ruble to $1.11; and for 1972, at an exchange rate of 1.21 rubles to the dollar.
[b]Soviet exports plus imports.
[c]Soviet exports minus imports. Soviet deficit (−), surplus (+). The USSR shows a trade surplus with Cuba for every year except 1960 and 1961.

early 1970s, Moscow was concentrating its aid efforts on Chile and Peru.

There is, however, a vast difference between the Soviet Union's highly publicized economic aid commitments and the actual transfer of resources. The economic value of Soviet aid commitments is substantially reduced as a result of price discrimination and particularly the low level of aid deliveries. Soviet aid deliveries at the end of 1971 amounted to $3.6 billion, or less than half of their commitments. The signing of an agreement has often been followed by time-consuming feasibility studies and pilot projects. Delays and inefficient implementation have also accounted for low deliveries. Sometimes the goods supplied were not suited to local conditions, or were deficient in design, quality, and spare parts. Scarcity of local currencies for projects, and difficulties in dealing with Moscow's cumbersome, inefficient state trading bureaucracy also slowed aid deliveries. Chile, for example, announced two credits in 1967 totalling $97 million to finance the construction of complete factories and the import of machinery and equipment. Four years later, the credits still had not been used. Other Latin American and Third World countries have had similar experiences. Despite well-advertised economic aid commitments and boasts of "fraternal and selfless assistance," Moscow's actual resource transfers to the developing countries are surprisingly low.

Soviet economic assistance to the developing countries fluctuates greatly from year to year. It rose from $194 million in 1970 to $886 million in 1971, but fell off to $618 million in 1972. Soviet leaders seem to have become aware of the limitations of economic aid as a political instrument. Such assistance often proves ineffective or counterproductive; it by no means guarantees lasting good will, and sometimes leads to embarrassing involvement in local or regional disputes; and the political pay-off can be shortlived or incommensurate with the investment. Russian caution in extending aid to Latin America has been influenced by economic difficulties at home, scarcity of foreign exchange, and the burden of other costly foreign commitments, such as in the Middle East.

TABLE 4

Soviet Economic Credits and Grants[a] Authorized
For Developing Countries by Geographical Area, 1954-72

(in millions of US dollars)

Years	Africa		Asia		Latin America		Middle East		Total
	Amount	Percent	Amount	Percent	Amount	Percent	Amount	Percent	
1965	28	15	66	34	15	8	84	44	193
1966	77	6	660	53	85	7	422	34	1,244
1967	9	3	5	2	97[b]	31	200	64	311
1968	0	0	194	52	2	1	178	48	374
1969	135	28	20	4	20	4	301	63	476
1970	51	26	11	6	56	29	76	39	194
1971	192	22	214	24	62[b]	7	418	47	886
1972	0	0	195	32	181[b]	29	242	39	618
Cumulative									
1954–1964	760	19	1,814	45	30	1	1,429	35	4,033
1965–1972	492	11	1,365	32	518	12	1,921	45	4,296
1954–1972	1,252	15	3,179	38	548	7	3,350	40	8,329

Source: US Department of State, Bureau of Intelligence and Research, Communist States and Developing Countries: Aid and Trade in 1972 (June 15, 1973).

[a] Only five percent of economic aid represents grants.

[b] These figures differ from State Department data as a result of upward adjustments in Soviet aid to Chile based on official Chilean figures.

Note: The sum of the regional percentages may not add up to 100 percent due to rounding.

Moscow is showing an increasing interest in providing economic and technical assistance for the exploitation of Latin America's raw materials and energy reserves. In accordance with Marxist-Leninist doctrine, the power of "imperialism" (that is, the United States) is due to its control over the raw materials of the colonial and semicolonial countries of the Third World. The Soviet leadership apparently believes it possible seriously to weaken the United States by encouraging the confiscation of American mining and industrial investments. The aim is not to gain control over Latin American resources for its own use or even to prevent the United States and other Western powers from having access to them. The main purpose is to dislodge the West from direct ownership and control of raw materials and energy resources. Moscow encourages the process by posing as a disinterested friend and shield against "imperialist" retaliation. This does not mean that Latin American nationalists are agents or stooges manipulated at Moscow's will. They are independent actors with whom the Soviet Union attempts to align itself to the detriment of the United States. Nevertheless, Moscow's alliance with Latin America nationalism is uneasy, as can be seen from its relations with Castro (prior to 1968) and Peru under the Velasco regime.

The USSR is also attempting to make its aid programs more efficient than the past. This has led to more careful joint planning and execution of aid projects with recipient countries. In the future, a selective Soviet involvement in the joint production of raw materials, the exchange of raw materials for foreign aid, and even the establishment of partnerships in raw materials processing should be anticipated. Despite low levels of aid at present, Moscow is striving for closer economic relations with the Latin American countries. Moscow may believe that a well-coordinated and executed program of economic penetration will lead to lasting political influence in Latin America, although it is by no means certain that this would be the outcome. In the past, dealings with the Soviet Union and exposure to life in the Socialist countries has not necessarily led to lasting friendship.

4

Soviet Espionage and Subversion

Despite Moscow's emphasis on peaceful coexistence and normal diplomatic relations, the Soviet Union continues to be actively involved in a wide range of secret operations in Latin America and around the world. Resumption of diplomatic relations with the majority of Latin American countries in the 1960s and early 1970s enabled Moscow vastly to expand its subversive and intelligence operations directed from its embassies and other official missions.

In the 1950s, when the Soviet Union had few embassies in Latin America, Soviet embassy officials were being expelled from one country or another every two or three years for involvement in espionage and subversive activities. Since 1968, the increase in the number of Soviet embassies and official missions has been accompanied by a discernible increase in the rate of expulsions. Soviet officials are now being declared *persona non grata* by one or two countries each year. From 1945 to 1973, some 80 Soviet diplomats and other officials were expelled by nine Latin American countries. An additional number of Soviet officials, which one source estimates at 20, were asked to leave under special arrangement with the Soviet government because their meddling

26

had become too obvious.[17] In the 1968-73 period alone, 63 Soviet officials were declared *persona non grata.* Uruguay expelled three in September 1968; Mexico, two in January 1969; Argentina, two in November 1970; Ecuador, three in July 1971; Mexico, five in March 1971; Bolivia, 25 in March 1972;[18] Colombia, three in August 1972; and Chile, 20 in September 1973.[19] The expelled Soviet officials included diplomats, nondiplomatic embassy personnel (cooks, technicians, trade and military officers), and representatives of such official agencies as Tass, *Izvestiya,* Intourist, and Radio Moscow. Thus, the postwar total of Soviet official representatives expelled or asked to leave now exceeds 100, with the majority of expulsions occurring recently—at the end of the 1960s and in the early 1970s.

Latin American governments have accused Soviet diplomats of such illegal activities as incitement to strike, involvement in student riots and attempted *coups d'état,* recruitment and training of local agents, distribution of hostile propaganda, financing terrorism and espionage, and training urban guerrillas. The Soviet Union is not alone, of course, among the advanced countries in conducting espionage operations. But the vast and growing scale of Soviet KGB (the secret intelligence and police organization) operations—its techniques of bribery, torture, murder, kidnapping, sabotage, and disinformation — are without parallel in Western countries. Both the scale and effectiveness of KGB operations in Latin America have increased markedly in recent years, with Moscow taking full advantage of the new opportunities afforded by the expanded Soviet official presence. After successful consolidation of the Soviet position in Cuba, the Soviet Union reorganized and strengthened its intelligence and propaganda network in the Western Hemisphere. Soviet KGB officers on assignment in the region are now younger, better educated, more cosmopolitan, and

[17]*El Siglo* (Bogota), April 24, 1971.

[18]*Reuters* (La Paz), March 29, 1972. Another 94 dependents of these Soviet officials left Bolivia in April 1972. The Bolivian government stated that the expelled Soviet officials were guilty of "interference in Bolivia's internal affairs."

[19]Expulsion of the 20 Soviet officials more or less coincided with Moscow's decision to suspend diplomatic relations.

TABLE 5

Soviet Official Representatives[a]
Declared *Persona Non Grata*
For Espionage and Subversive Activities
in Latin America, 1946-73

Date	Country	Name
September 1973	Chile[b]	Aleksey Afanaskin
		Nikolay Diakov
		Boris Demine
		Viktor Efremov
		Guerman Gorelov
		Mikhail Isaev
		Nikolay Kotchanov
		Aleksey Kourassov
		Vasiliy Vis Logousov
		Valery Nozarov
		Nikolay Perets
		Vladimir Poliakov
		Aleksey Pozniakov
		Viktor Segov
		Valery Sergueev
		Viktor Sossov
		Vasiliy Stepanov
		Aleksandr. Tchernosvitov
		Viktor Voronets
		Vasiliy Zakharov
August 1972	Colombia	Gennadiy S. Karpov
		Georgiy A. Khurbatov
		Boris F. Mantyukov
April 1972	Bolivia[c]	Yuriy A. Sakhnin
		Igor Y. Sholokhov
July 1971	Ecuador	Robespierre N. Filatov
		Valentin A. Goluzin
		Anatoliy M. Shadrin

TABLE 5 (Continued)

Date	Country	Name
March 1971	Mexico	Aleksandr. V. Bolshakov Dmitriy A. Dyakonov Boris P. Kolomyakov Oleg M. Nechiporenko Boris N. Voskoboynikov
November 1970	Argentina	Yuriy L. Mamontov Yuriy I. Ryabov
January 1969	Mexico	Viktor N. Mednikov Vladimir Y. Serveyev
September 1968	Uruguay	Viktor N. Glotov Anatoli I. Ladygin Georgiy G. Matukhin
October 1966	Uruguay	Nikolay I. Ivanov Vladimir F. Shvets Sergey A. Yangaykin Aleksey A. Zudin
April 1966	Brazil	Vitaliy I. Kobysh
December 1964	Colombia	Mikhail I. Kolesnikov Aleksandr D. Opekunov
January 1961	Uruguay	Mikhail K. Samoylov
April 1959	Argentina	Nikolay A. Belous Dmitriy A. Dyakonov Vasiliy G. Ivashov Konstantin P. Monakhov
April 1959	Mexico	Nikolay V. Aksenov Nikolay M. Remizov

TABLE 5 (Continued)

Date	Country	Name
June 1956	Argentina	Aleksandr D. Morozov
June 1952	Venezuela	Mikhail S. Alyabynev Lev V. Krylov

[a] Includes Soviet diplomats, other nondiplomatic embassy personnel (such as technicians and trade officials), and representatives of official Soviet agencies such as Tass, Intourist, and Radio Moscow.

[b] Some 12 of these Soviet officials were employed in a Russian-built factory near Valparaiso, and were military officers involved in training urban guerrillas; the remainder were Soviet technicians in the same factory. All were expelled by the Chilean junta soon after September 11, 1973, along with 12 dependents.

[c] The two Soviet Embassy officials were declared *persona non grata* for involvement in subversive activities, and 23 other Soviet officials were also asked to leave the country. Another 94 dependents of these officials also left the country during April 1972, bringing the total "reduction in force" of Soviet officials and dependents to 119.

Sources: New York Times, Washington Post, Miami Herald, various Latin American newspapers, and official sources.

fluent in Spanish. They are far more sophisticated and effective than their predecessors in the early postwar period.

Moscow's Cuban Base

In the early 1960s, Moscow's principal espionage center in the Caribbean was located in Cuba, where approximately 400 Soviet intelligence officers were sent to train and support revolutionary groups throughout the Hemisphere.[20] In mid-1961, the Cuban intelligence service (General Directorate of Intelligence, or DGI) was set up with the assistance of the Soviet Union, and maintained its autonomy until 1967, when it came under direct Soviet control. The DGI now finances only the training, arms purchases, and other activities of revolutionary groups that have Moscow's approval.

During the 1960s, the DGI was divided into Central and South American sections, each responsible for directing revolutionary activities and intelligence operations within its geographic area. An estimated 2,500 Latin Americans (and some North Americans) have been trained in subversive operations and revolutionary violence at various Cuban centers since the DGI was organized. The techniques of guerrilla warfare and urban terrorism are taught at special Cuban schools, where fledgling revolutionaries acquire knowledge of weapons handling, manufacture of explosives, military tactics, combat engineering, demolition, and sabotage.

During Raul Castro's visit to the USSR in April-May 1970, Soviet officials urged that the DGI be reorganized and expanded so that additional DGI officials could be sent overseas to replace Foreign Ministry personnel in various embassy posts.[21] Moscow argued that the primary mission of the Cuban government abroad was to gather intelligence and support national liberation movements, which was the responsibility of the DGI and not the

---

[20] *New York Times*, December 7, 1970.

[21] Brian Crozier, *Soviet Pressures in the Caribbean*, Conflict Studies No. 35 (London: Institute for the Study of Conflict, 1973), p. 14.

Foreign Ministry. Despite strong resistance by Raul Roa, the Cuban Foreign Minister, the Soviet recommendations were followed after Raul Castro returned to Cuba.

Cuban diplomats began to be replaced by DGI officers in December 1970, and this process continued throughout 1971. Several Cuban ambassadors were also removed for ideological and personal weaknesses uncovered by the DGI. In Havana, Manuel Pineiro Losada, the Director General of Intelligence, was replaced by Jose Mendez Cominchez, a pro-Soviet nominee of Raul Castro, and other anti-Soviet DGI officers were also removed. Major policy guidelines for Cuba's intelligence service are now established by the Central Committee of the CPSU. A Soviet KGB official supervises the implementation of Moscow's directives within the DGI, reviews all annual DGI operational plans down to the section level, and screens sensitive operations involving the placement of key agents.[22]

It is well known among Cuban intelligence officers that the KGB has penetrated Cuba's DGI and actively recruits agents from among the 60 Cuban officers trained by the Russians each year. This inevitably increases the reliability of Soviet control over the Cuban intelligence organization. A total of about 550 Cuban intelligence officers have received ten months' training in two Soviet intelligence schools in and near Moscow since 1964.[23]

Cuba's intelligence operations abroad are so closely coordinated with those of the Soviet KGB that the Cuban DGI effectively serves as an arm of Soviet intelligence. This suits Soviet purposes in Latin America, where intelligence and subversive operations can be carried out by the Cubans without exposing Moscow's hand. Under the Allende government, for example, Moscow was privy to all of the intelligence gathered by the large DGI staff based in the Cuban Embassy in Santiago.

[22] *Ibid.*, p.16.
[23] *Ibid.*

Moscow's Base in Mexico

Since the early 1950s, Mexico City has served as the major support base for Soviet intelligence operations in the United States and the Caribbean (including Central America and northern South America). At the end of 1970, an estimated 120 Soviet personnel were employed in the Soviet Embassy in Mexico City.[24] This number includes the wives of Soviet diplomats, who have regularly assigned duties within the Embassy complex as secretaries, bookkeepers, telex operators, and kitchen help, and sometimes as KGB agents.[25] The limited scope of official Soviet-Mexican relations obviously does not justify so large a staff, and at least 40 of the Soviet male diplomats in Mexico City are considered to be intelligence officers. Until recently, Moscow carefully avoided activities directly offensive to the Mexican government, which has found it politically expedient to tolerate the large Soviet presence.

The Soviet Embassy in Mexico City engages in a wide range of subversive activities throughout the Caribbean. These include: providing funds and guidance to local Communist parties and groups; distributing anti-US propaganda and literature; recruiting leftists, students, and Russian emigres for Soviet intelligence; selecting students for travel scholarships to the Soviet Union and Soviet bloc countries, and for study in Moscow at the Patrice Lumumba Friendship University; maintaining contact with local leftist and Marxist revolutionary groups; engaging in espionage and intelligence gathering; attempting to influence important university students and labor leaders; acting as a transfer point for Soviet agents to and from the Caribbean and the United States.

Despite its toleration of Soviet subversive operations, Mexico has not escaped Moscow's political interference. On March 21,

[24]*New York Times,* December 7, 1970.
[25]Such as Lydia Nechiporenko, wife of Oleg Nechiporenko, who was expelled by the Mexican government in March 1971. Lydia Nechiporenko was assigned a full-time job within the Soviet Embassy by the KGB. Barrow, *op. cit.,* p. 233.

1971, five KGB officers masquerading as Soviet diplomats were expelled by the Mexican government for helping to finance and organize a revolutionary movement called the Revolutionary Action Movement (MAR). The MAR was organized in 1968 by Fabricio Gomez Souza, a KGB agent recruited in Mexico City in 1963.[26] Boris N. Vosboynikov, a KGB officer posing as the Soviet Cultural Attache in Mexico City, chose a number of Mexican students in 1968-70 for training as Moscow's Patrice Lumumba University to become a nucleus of pro-Soviet activities upon their return to Mexico. The KGB also arranged for a group of Moscow-trained and other Mexican students to receive instruction in guerrilla warfare in North Korea, so as to avoid the appearance of Soviet involvement. The fledgling guerrillas returned to Mexico, joined the MAR, and were arrested by the Mexican government for "conspiracy and inciting rebellion, criminal association, armed robbery, homicide, unauthorized possession of arms, forgery, and the use of forged public documents."[27] The captured guerrillas confessed that they were trained in sabotage, terrorism, robbery, and guerrilla tactics in 1969 and 1970 at a North Korean military base in the vicinity of Pyongyang. Because of direct KGB involvement in the organization of the MAR, the Mexican government expelled the five Soviet diplomats in order to emphasize the seriousness with which it viewed Moscow's support of the Mexican guerrillas.

This was not the first time that the KGB had been involved in subversive activities in Mexico. A few years prior to his expulsion, Boris Voskoboynikov was responsible for directing Communist youth groups in demonstrations against the Mexican government. Voskoboynikov and other KGB officers organized and financed a group of disciplined Communist students and youths who formed part of the "shock brigades" that initiated the tragic confrontation in Mexico City between government troops and 6,000 young people on October 2, 1968, a few days before the opening of the 1968 Olympic Games. Some 28 persons (26 civilians and two

[26]*Ibid.*, pp. 230-252, for details.
[27]*Statement*, Attorney General's Office, Mexico City, March 16, 1971.

soldiers) were killed in the ensuing battle between the student demonstrators and the troops.

Communist propaganda, political agitation, and espionage activities often increase markedly after a country establishes relations with the Soviet Union. In Colombia, for example, Communist labor agitation and indoctrination,[28] press infiltration,[29] and the distribution of propaganda materials[30] rose sharply during 1972. Soviet diplomats were accused of providing money and other assistance to local Communists. In August 1972, Colombia's Foreign Minister expelled three officials of the Soviet Embassy in Bogota for "intervening" in the internal affairs of the country.[31] There is also evidence that the KGB, using *Novosti* and Tass as covers, was strengthening Soviet espionage operations in Colombia and Venezuela in the early 1970s.[32]

In July 1971, Ecuador ousted three Russian officials for involvement in domestic labor problems.[32a] The officials — Anatoliy M. Shadrin, a political officer, Robespierre Filatov, First Secretary of the Soviet Embassy, and Valentin A. Goluzin — were reliably reported to be the KGB agents who supplied funds to the Marxist-dominated Confederation of Ecuadorian Workers (CTE). The CTE used the funds for a general strike that was supposed to be coordinated with a military coup by a pro-Moscow military faction. In this instance, the Ecuadorian government did not break relations with the Soviet Union. Similar episodes occurred in Uruguay in 1971 and Colombia in 1973. While there is little evidence of outside funding or direction of the urban terrorist Tupamaros, relations between the Tupamaros, the local pro-Moscow Communist Party, and Soviet and Cuban officials in Uruguay were suspiciously close. In June 1971, President Jorge Pacheco-Areco warned the Soviet Union that diplomatic relations might be

[28]*EFE* (Madrid), September 21, 1972.
[29]*El Siglo* (Bogota), September 14, 1972.
[30]*Ibid.*
[31]*UPI* (Bogota), August 5, 1972.
[32]*El Mundo* (Caracas), February 20, 1971.
[32a]*Christian Science Monitor*, July 10, 1971.

broken. In Colombia, the government seriously considered severing relations with the USSR in 1973 after intercepting Soviet funds destined for Colombian guerrillas.[33]

These recent instances of Soviet complicity in illegal and anti-government activities raised a storm of protest in Latin America. But despite the disruptive potential inherent in diplomatic relations with the Soviet Union, most countries still consider the anticipated political and economic advantages worth the risks. Moreover, anti-American nationalism in Latin America continues to see the establishment of ties with the Soviet Union as an act of defiance against the United States.

On the other hand, the subversive dangers involved in increased Soviet propaganda and intelligence activities, while very real, should not be exaggerated. At least half of the Soviet intelligence effort based in Mexico, for example, is directed against the United States. Furthermore, Moscow is selective in its clandestine support for terrorist and guerrilla movements, and makes every effort not to compromise its image of a "normal" and "businesslike" diplomatic partner. Soviet leaders are pragmatic, and emphasize a "correct" or noninterventionist posture wherever revolutionary violence and subversive initiatives show little prospect of success. In such circumstances, the Soviets concentrate on manipulating and influencing "respectable" political individuals and groups in an attempt to capitalize on anti-American nationalist sentiment.

[33]*UPI* (Bogota), September 30, 1973. In April 1968, Colombian police, alerted by Mexican authorities, seized $100,000 from two Communist couriers. They had received the money in Mexico City from Nikolai Sergeevich Leonov, a KGB officer. See Barron, *op. cit.*, p. 256.

5

Moscow's Support for Revolutionary Violence

Despite a widespread impression to the contrary, Moscow is involved in sponsoring terrorism or guerrilla warfare in many parts of the world, including Latin America.[34] The provision of arms, money, and training to numerous revolutionary groups is an element in Moscow's worldwide strategy of expanding its influence and ultimately establishing client states in the Third World. Revolutionary violence is also supported where necessary to establish Moscow's revolutionary credentials, particularly when challenged by Peking and ultraleftist groups.

Soviet Clandestine Operations

Overt support for guerrilla war or urban terrorism is generally avoided so as to preserve Moscow's carefully cultivated and reassuring image of normality. The clandestine nature of Soviet assistance to revolutionary groups, which in Latin America mainly takes the form of support for Cuba's revolutionary ventures, makes comprehensive evidence impossible. Still, more is known about

[34]Brian Crozier, "The Soviet Involvement in Violence," *Soviet Analyst*, vol. 1, no. 11 (July 20, 1972), p. 4.

Soviet activities in Latin America than elsewhere as a result of recent disclosures by defectors from the Cuban intelligence apparatus, including Orlando Castro Hidalgo and Gerardo Peraza.[35]

The differing revolutionary interests of Cuba and the Soviet Union were a bone of contention between the two regimes throughout the 1960s. Moscow and the orthodox Communist parties gave a qualified endorsement to Cuba's strategy of armed struggle in the early part of the decade. The Soviet Union even supported a number of Cuban-backed guerrilla groups in order to retain some measure of influence over the direction of the Latin American revolutionary movement. By the mid-1960s, however, prospects for gaining power through revolutionary violence had dimmed, and overt association with guerrilla movements was rejected as self-defeating and contrary to current Soviet interests. US military intervention during the Dominican revolt of 1965 demonstrated the strength and effectiveness of Washington's determination to prevent further Communist encroachments in the Caribbean. As a result, Moscow gradually disengaged from the continental revolution and reverted to a more limited and cautious strategy. Thereafter, the Soviet Union moved rapidly to establish normal relations with various Latin American countries as the most effective available means of expanding its influence. As their revolutionary views and tactics diverged, relations between Cuba and the Soviet Union became increasingly strained.

By the early 1970s, however, Soviet efforts to gain control over Cuban foreign policy had been largely successful. Although Moscow was unable to manipulate the Cuban Communist Party apparatus or threaten military intervention, as was possible in Eastern Europe, Cuba's acute economic dependence on Soviet trade and aid nevertheless gave the Russians considerable

[35]Orlando Castro Hidalgo, *Spy for Fidel* (Miami: Seemann Publishing, 1971). Orlando Castro Hidalgo was a DGI official in Paris at the time of his defection in April 1969. Gerardo Peraza, a DGI official in Cuba's London Embassy, defected in September 1971 and fled Britain for asylum in the United States in November.

leverage, which they used against Castro with evident effectiveness. Moscow threatened to cut off all economic aid and strategic imports unless Castro refrained from criticizing Soviet foreign policy, attempting to discredit Moscow-line Communist parties, and launching guerrilla actions in various countries without prior consultation with Moscow. Indeed, Castro was required to sign a secret agreement binding himself to support the Soviet line.[36] A more recent Cuban intelligence defector, Gerardo Peraza, reported in September 1971 that the Soviet KGB in Havana compelled Raul Castro in 1970 to purge all anti-Soviet officers in the Cuban Directorate of Intelligence (DGI).[37]

The Russians, in turn, have agreed to finance those DGI operations that have their approval, such as the training of the Bolivian Army of National Liberation (ELN) in Chile. Various Bolivian officials have claimed that the ELN was reorganized in Chile for the purpose of overthrowing the Bolivian regime, and with the knowledge and logistical support of the Allende government.[38] According to Peraza, DGI training activities were permitted in Chile because Allende was prepared to allow the Cubans to use their newly-established Santiago Embassy as their main intelligence and revolutionary center in the Western Hemisphere.[39] Fidel Castro sent intelligence agents to Santiago immediately after Allende's election. By the end of 1970, two high-ranking officers, Juan Carretero Ibanca and Luis Fernandez Ona, were permanently installed in the Chilean capital. They headed a team of six Cuban officers whose first priority was the reorganization of Allende's personal guard (Grupo de Amigos Personales, or GAP) and the Chilean security services.[40]

---

[36]See the testimony of Orlando Castro Hidalgo, *Hearings before the Internal Security Subcommittee, Committee of the Judiciary,* US Senate, 91st Congress, Part 20, October 16, 1969 (Washington: US Government Printing Office, 1970), pp. 1425-1426.

[37]Crozier, *op. cit.*

[38]*Agence France Presse* (La Paz), June 20, 1972.

[39]Crozier, *op. cit.*

[40]*Daily Telegraph,* September 16, 1973.

Cuba also provided military equipment and training for Marxist paramilitary formations in Chile. These formations were strengthened by contingents of revolutionaries from Argentina, Bolivia, Brazil, Cuba, Mexico, Peru, and other countries. Soon after these foreigners arrived in Chile, they were provided with false identity documents and many were given jobs in state enterprises and government departments. Cuban officials maintained close contact with the Chilean ultraleftist and revolutionary exile groups and attempted to create a new Latin American anti-imperialist front based in Chile.[41]

To offset Soviet influence over Cuba's intelligence service (DGI), Fidel Castro set up a new organization in 1970, the Directorate of National Liberation (DLN), and staffed it with the anti-Soviet staff dismissed from the DGI, including Manuel Pineiro Losada (former DGI chief), who was appointed Director. The DLN planned various operations in Latin America that Moscow disapproved of, the most important of which was the Chilean operation. Castro suffered a serious reverse as a result of the overthrow of the Allende regime. Chile's military junta immediately expelled 150 Cuban officials and dependents, dismantled the guerrilla training camps and intelligence center, and broke diplomatic relations. In a desperate bid to bolster the morale of President Allende and to offer Cuban assistance in the event of an armed confrontation, Castro even dispatched Manuel Pineiro and Carlos Rafael Rodriquez (Vice Prime Minister) to Santiago in August 1973, one month before the military coup;[42] but to no avail.

The serious deterioration of the Cuban economy in recent years has severely restricted the revenues available for financing Castro's revolutionary adventures. Cuba, therefore turned to North Korea for financial and military aid.[43] At the end of 1970, Chile and

[41]*UPI* (Washington), December 20, 1971.
[42]See Fidel Castro's letter to Salvador Allende dated July 29, 1973, and published in *Libro Blanco del Cambio de Gobierno* (Santiago: 1973), pp. 101-102.
[43]Crozier, *op. cit.*

North Korea agreed to establish diplomatic relations. North Korea then opened a trade mission in Santiago in May 1971; and as a result, a North Korean guerrilla training mission installed in Cuba since 1970 was transferred to Chile. The North Koreans agreed to train the paramilitary forces of the Chilean Socialist Party (part of the Popular Unity ruling coalition), which were distinct from the larger forces of the Movement of the Revolutionary Left (MIR).[44] Both MIR and Socialist Party extremists were committed to creating an irreversible revolutionary situation and then forcing a confrontation with the security forces. Throughout 1973, the Socialist shock brigades employed violence on a growing scale to intimidate the democratic opposition.[45] This was one of the major factors responsible for the military coup.

The Cubans and North Koreans have different approaches to revolutionary violence. In Chile, the Cubans favored bombings and assassinations, while avoiding a direct engagement with the state security forces. North Korea recommended more aggressive tactics, such as large-scale sabotage, in order to provoke the armed forces into premature action. The Russians were opposed to the dangerously provocative revolutionary violence launched by the Chilean ultraleft, over which they had no control, and generally avoided overt involvement in the internal affairs of the country. They played a double game. They gave support to the cautious, disciplined pro-Moscow Chilean Communist Party (also part of the ruling coalition), which advocated a gradual approach to the seizure of power, and opposed both the MIR's violent seizures of farms and factories and the illegal acts of the Socialist Party extremists. At the same time, Moscow did nothing to stop the training of MIR guerrillas by the Cuban DGI. The Russians also used Cuba to infiltrate large amounts of Soviet and Czechoslovak arms into Chile for use by the ultraleftists, and even directed Soviet army officers to train a hard core of worker-revolutionaries in urban guerrilla tactics.[46] While officially criticizing the armed struggle, Moscow

---

[44]*Ibid.*
[45]*UPI* (Santiago), February 1, 1973.
[46]*Washington Star-News*, January 14, 1974.

apparently hoped to maintain some influence with the extreme left by selective support of the revolution.

In general, Moscow finances only those operations of the Cuban DGI where local revolutionary groups can be persuaded to accept united front tactics and overall direction from local pro-Soviet Communist parties. Where socalled liberation movements are in conflict with the orthodox Communist parties, the Russians, as pragmatists, much prefer to see them under Cuban control rather than run the risk that they fall under Chinese control. Soviet officials usually avoid overt involvement in support of revolutionary activities. Soviet money used to finance revolutionary violence is often channeled through Cuba and the East European countries, whose espionage organizations are entirely under Soviet control.[47]

Cuba's Support for Insurgency

Cuba continues to be the main base for the export of revolution to Latin America, although on a very much reduced scale as compared to the 1960s. The failure of the armed struggle abroad, economic difficulties and social unrest at home, and increased Soviet leverage in Havana have forced Castro to mend his fences with the Kremlin. With evident reluctance and strong reservations, Castro has accepted Moscow's current peaceful coexistence line and its stress on the evolutionary path to socialism. Castro's foreign policy is now closely aligned with that of the Soviet Union, and he is showing more interest in breaking out of diplomatic isolation, resuming economic ties with Cuba's neighbors, and increasing his diplomatic influence in Hemispheric affairs. This *volte-face* was bitterly attacked by Latin America's ultraleftist forces. It raised doubts about Castro's revolutionary credentials, and revealed the emptiness of his inflated pretensions to be the *líder máximo* of the Latin American revolution.

[47]See Barron, *op. cit.*

Nevertheless, Castro has not completely abandoned his efforts to export Cuban-style armed revolution to Latin America, as Cuban support for revolutionary violence in Chile during the Allende regime makes perfectly clear. Castro-inspired guerrillas or terrorists in Venezuela, Colombia, Guatemala, the Dominican Republic, Haiti, Mexico, Puerto Rico, and the West Indies continue to receive some sporadic support from Cuba — money, arms, propaganda material, and especially training. Cuban instructors are still training Latin American guerrillas in urban and rural insurgency at a half dozen camps in Cuba.[48] Despite Castro's best revolutionary efforts, however, no government in the Western Hemisphere has been seriously threatened by Cuba-supported guerrillas, with the possible exception of Chile. Today, armed revolutionaries are mainly an irritant, and nowhere pose a major security threat. Most governments consider indigenous terrorist groups, some of which maintain contact with Cuba, to be potentially more dangerous and disruptive.

Che Guevara's disastrous failure in Bolivia, and his death in October 1967, dramatized the collapse of the rural guerrilla movement in Latin America. This fiasco was only one of a series of defeats inflicted on the guerrillas after 1965 in Peru, Venezuela, Colombia, and Guatemala, where the rebel movements in the countryside were isolated and generally rendered ineffective. The "objective conditions" (willingness of peasants to lend support, existence of unpopular governments, and so forth) apparently have not yet "ripened" to the point where they could be successfully exploited by determined leaders. Moreover, the guerrillas were almost invariably inept and isolated from the local inhabitants by insuperable barriers of language, class, and culture; they were poorly financed by the hard-pressed Cuban Treasury; they were badly supported by traditional Communist parties and faction-ridden left-wing groups in urban centers; and they faced armies increasingly well-trained and equipped for counterinsurgency by the United States.

[48]Testimony of State Department officials, *Hearings Before the Committee on Foreign Relations,* US Senate, 92nd Congress, September 16, 1971 (Washington: US Government Printing Office, 1971), p.9.

Urban Guerrillas

In any event, the failure of rural-based insurgency has led to a shift in emphasis to urban terrorism. Despite Castro's characterization of the cities as the "graveyard of revolutionaries," revolutionary violence has mounted steadily in the urban centers of Latin America since 1967-68. The shift to urban terrorism has not, of course, meant complete abandonment of rural guerrilla operations. The latter are still active, albeit on a reduced scale, in Venezuela, Colombia, Guatemala, and even Mexico. The new emphasis on urban guerrillas after Guevara's death seems to be a tactical maneuver designed to put local governments on the defensive. Guerrilla leaders continue to argue that the fate of the revolution ultimately will be decided in the countryside. In the meantime, however, the indirect path through urban violence promises initial success and momentum.

To some extent, the guerrillas operate under more favorable conditions in the cities than on the countryside. The cadres are drawn mainly from urban intellectuals, university students, and professionals who are at home in the city and indistinguishable from other urban dwellers. They find support among radical elements of the clergy, such as the "Third World" movement, from ultraleftist parties, and the extremist wings of the labor movement.

In Latin America, urban terrorists have been most active in Argentina, Chile, Colombia, Dominican Republic, Guatemala, Uruguay, and Venezuela; and less conspicuous in Central America, the Spanish-speaking West Indies, and Mexico. Cuba has given diplomatic and propaganda support as well as some training to the Castro-supported "independentistas" in Puerto Rico. There is no firm evidence that Black Power nationalism in the English-speaking Caribbean, which shares many of the nationalist aims of the Cuban revolution, receives support from Cuba or from the Soviet Union.

Urban guerrillas generally lack ideological or programmatic cohesion beyond the standard leftist slogans and themes. But their lack of singleminded dedication to a common cause does not render them any less disruptive or dangerous. The basic aims of the urban terrorists are to engender a general sense of insecurity amid the breakdown of law and order; to put a government on the defensive and demonstrate its impotence; to isolate a regime by forcing it to resort to counterproductive repression; to gain publicity by spectacular acts (occupying villages, kidnapping foreign diplomats, robbing banks); and, in general, to inflate the revolutionary image. They seek to destroy the electoral process where it exists, polarize political forces, and create conditions for civil strife that will culminate in the overthrow of the existing regime.

Latin America's urban guerrillas receive only sporadic material support from Cuba, and depend mainly on robbery or the ransoming of kidnapped victims for funds, arms, and other equipment. Like the rural insurgents before them, they have not been able to mobilize widespread popular support. Their methods have been too violent, and their aims too obscure. The showpiece successes of the urban terrorists reflect not so much guerrilla strength as the universal difficulties of policing cities.

Revolutionary Prospects

Even if immediate prospects for the success of rural and urban-based insurgency movements in most of the Caribbean and South America are meager, the picture could change in the 1970s. A growing Soviet military presence — particularly an increase in the visibility of Soviet naval power — in Latin America could contribute to a subtle but progressive change in the entire political-psychological environment in which revolution grows. In the past, the proximate and unrivaled power of the United States dampened the hopes of Communist revolutionaries that success (in the form of the overthrow of the existing government and the seizure of power) could be maintained, once that has been achieved. In the future, however, the presence of a rival superpower might well change this perception of the odds.

The fragmentation of the left in Latin America is the legacy of numerous setbacks, notably the failure of the prolonged guerrilla campaigns in Venezuela and Guatemala. The guerrilla movements in Guatemala and Venezuela failed because the insurgents were unable to obtain an indispensable minimum of peasant cooperation. In future campaigns, they may be more fortunate. Not all governments in the area can safely count on the massive peasant support against extremist guerrillas that Venezuela, Costa Rica, and Mexico can. And even in Mexico, this may not be true for all parts of the country.

Moreover, Latin American revolutionaries and leftist politicians are remarkably persistent and resilient. New hope of success inspired by a strong nationalist tide and a "protective" Soviet presence might be enough to induce them to overcome their sectarian differences and form a successful united front, as they did in Chile for the 1970 election. It would be a mistake, however, to assume that the pro-Soviet Communist parties—and their mentors in Moscow—are now dedicated exclusively to the peaceful road to power. In the event of a setback in East-West relations, or an improvement in the prospects for revolutionary violence, they could quickly switch to more active support for the armed revolutionary path to power.

6

Relations with Latin American Communist Parties

Moscow's association with the Latin American Communist parties reaches back to the Russian revolution. During the Stalinist period, the Latin American Communist parties were monolithic organizations, with strong internal discipline and undeviating loyalty to Moscow. But even before the death of Stalin, the Marxist Left began to fragment, and the post-World War II crisis of world communism deeply split the Communist movement in the Western Hemisphere. The Cuban revolution led to a further splintering of the Marxist Left and the spawning of dissident Communist groups that contested the revolutionary leadership of the orthodox parties.

These dissident Communist groups, while calling themselves Marxist-Leninist, are frequently antagonistic to the local Communist parties and to Moscow. They accuse the Latin American Communist parties of not being genuinely revolutionary, and this is not an entirely ridiculous accusation. The Latin American Communist movement lacks a vigorous revolutionary tradition. On a continent racked by civil strife and insurrections, the record of the Communists has been remarkably quiescent. The revolt against the Brazilian government led by Luiz Prestes in 1935, and perhaps also

47

the Communist-inspired uprising in El Salvador in 1932, are the only major Communist attempts to seize power by force, although there have been instances of Communist participation in uprisings organized by non-Communist groups.

The lack of revolutionary fervor does not signify that the Communist parties of Latin America are democratic. They are totalitarian parties with a totalitarian organization and totalitarian mentality. They do not believe in democratic pluralism or in civil rights enjoyed in Western democracies. Whenever they have managed to share real power, as in Chile in 1946-47 and 1970-73, in Guatemala in 1954, and in Cuba from 1960 onward, their totalitarian character has immediately become evident in their behavior toward both allies and opponents.[49]

Strength of Latin American Communism

At the present time, Latin American communism is divided into four main parties or groups: the orthodox, pro-Moscow parties; the pro-Castro parties; the pro-Peking parties; and the independent parties or groups that refuse to follow the lead of Moscow, Peking, or Havana.

Communist Party membership in the 20 Latin American republics, the four English-speaking Caribbean states, and the French Departments of Martinique and Guadeloupe is estimated at 400,000 in 1973. A much larger number—perhaps three or four times—are Communist sympathizers or fellow travelers. The largest parties are to be found in Cuba (125,000), Chile (120,000),[50] Argentina (70,000), Uruguay (22,000), Mexico (15,000), Colombia (11,000), Venezuela (8,000), and Brazil (7,000). There are numerous front organizations of varying importance in each country that must also be taken into account when assessing the strength of communism.

[49]See Ernst Halperin, "Latin America," *Survey*, no. 54 (January 1965), pp. 154-155.

[50]These figures refer to the Chilean Communist Party before the military coup of September 11, 1973, which overthrew Allende's Marxist government, arrested the Communist Party leadership, and declared the Party illegal.

TABLE 6

Communist Party Membership
in Latin America, 1973[a]

Pro-Moscow parties	263,085
Pro-Peking parties	3,810
Pro-Castro parties	1,000[b]
Independents	10,675[c]
Cuba's Fidelista party	125,000
Undetermined	850
Total	404,420

[a]Includes estimates of the four English-speaking Caribbean states, plus Martinique and Guadeloupe.

[b]The precise strength of many Fidelista parties and groups is not known, and this may be a conservative estimate.

[c]Includes Trotskyites and other nonaffiliated dissident groups.

Source: World Strength of Communist Party Organizations (Washington: US Department of State, 1973); and Brian Crozier, ed., *Annual of Power and Conflict,* 1971 (London: Institute for the Study of Conflict, 1972).

Apart from Cuba, the strongest Communist parties in terms of membership and influence are to be found in Argentina, Chile, Uruguay, and Mexico. Prior to the September 1973 military coup, Chile had by far the strongest and best organized Communist Party in South America, as well as an ideologically unstable Socialist Party that was almost as strong. The Chilean Communists are staunchly loyal to Moscow; and their leader, Luis Corvalan, was for years the most outspoken advocate of Soviet interests in Latin America. The Chilean Communist Party (and the other parties of the Popular Unity Coalition) suffered a severe reverse as a result of the September 1973 military coup that overthrew the Allende regime, jailed the Party leadership (including Luis Corvalan), and declared the Party illegal. The small, splintered parties of Spanish-speaking Central America and the island republics are generally

weak and politically insignificant. Communist Party membership
and influence are negligible in the English-speaking Caribbean
states except for Guyana.[51]

In all of Central and South America, Communist parties enjoy
legal status only in Argentina, Colombia, Costa Rica, Ecuador,
Guyana, Mexico, Peru, Uruguay, and Venezuela, as well as in the
French territories of Martinique and Guadeloupe. Whether illegal
or legal, however, the Communist parties and their front groups
carry on extensive propaganda activities in most countries of the
area, and have infiltrated such key social groups as organized labor,
university students, and the intellectual elite. On the other hand,
they have made little headway in penetrating military and civilian
government circles.

Even in those countries where they are weak or illegal, the
Communist parties are a factor to be reckoned with. The few
thousand votes controlled by a Communist Party may swing an
election; its influence among university students may serve to start
or quell a riot; its trade union connections may be useful to the military dictator struggling to improve his image and win a civilian
following. The extraordinary opportunism and flexibility of the
Communist parties make it possible for their services to be bought
at a moderate price: a few jobs in a state-controlled trade union
bureaucracy, amnesty for imprisoned comrades, or permission to
publish a daily newspaper or periodical.[52] It has been precisely the
weakness of the Latin American Communist parties that has
enabled politicians to cooperate with them without courting disaster. Politicians wishing to shake off their Communist allies when
their usefulness has been exhausted have rarely found it difficult to
do so.

[51]The leader of Guyana's People's Progressive Party (PPP), Cheddi Jagan, is a
Moscow-line Communist; but the rank-and-file East Indian party member has
little interest in Communist ideology.

[52]See Halperin, *op. cit.*

Orthodox Pro-Soviet Parties

At present, Moscow-oriented parties exist in 20 of the 24 Latin American and English-speaking republics: Argentina, Bolivia, Brazil, Chile, Colombia, Costa Rica, Dominican Republic, Ecuador, El Salvador, Guatemala, Guyana, Haiti, Honduras, Mexico, Nicaragua, Panama, Paraguay, Peru, Uruguay, and Venezuela. These pro-Moscow parties depend on the Soviet Union for support and guidance, and ceaselessly strive to advance Soviet foreign policy interests, often at the expense of their own countries. This close identification with a foreign power is a major handicap and limits local Communist appeal. On the other hand, without Soviet material, moral, and ideological support, these generally weak and faction-ridden parties probably would not survive.

Most of the high and middle level leaders of the orthodox parties were trained and indoctrinated in the Soviet Union and Eastern Europe. They have been taught to defend and foster Moscow's interests in their own countries and to remain slavishly loyal through every twist of Soviet policy. In the period since World War II, they have made a considerable effort to distribute Soviet propaganda, arrange visits to the Soviet Union and Eastern Europe, and establish "friendship" organizations to propagandize the Soviet Union in their countries.[53] The most important function of Latin American Communist leaders for half a century has been to serve the interests of the Soviet Union.[54]

The orthodox parties reject the armed revolutionary path to power and adhere to the more cautious, flexible, essentially non-militant line prescribed by Moscow. In large part, the divergence in strategy and doctrine between the revolutionary and Moscow-line parties stems from differences in age, training, indoctrination, and association with the Soviet Union. Generally, the pro-Moscow

[53]Robert J. Alexander, "The Impact of the Sino-Soviet Split on Latin American Communism," in Donald L. Herman, ed., *The Communist Tide in Latin America* (Austin: University of Texas Press, 1972).
[54]*Ibid.*

leadership has been drawn from the property-owning middle class. They now tend to be middle-aged or older, and understandably lack enthusiasm for the idea of waging revolutionary warfare in rural areas or in the cities. Moreover, they are reluctant to jeopardize the varying degrees of respectability and influence they have gained within the labor movement, national and local governments, and political and intellectual circles of their respective countries.

Fidelista and Pro-Peking Parties

Cuba's Fidelista Party is the largest in the area and one of the few Communist parties in Latin America that follows a line more or less independent of Moscow or Peking, although since 1968 Castro has moved much closer to the pro-Soviet position on most domestic and international issues. A number of weak, faction-ridden Fidelista parties in the Dominican Republic, Nicaragua, Panama, Colombia, and elsewhere also accept Havana's leadership. In addition, Castro exercises considerable personal influence over a wide range of radical non-Communist parties in Latin America. Some Chilean Socialists (Salvador Allende was a close personal friend of Castro), the Chilean MIR, the Uruguyan Tupamaros, the Argentine People's Revolutionary Army (ERP), and the Bolivian National Liberation Army (ELN), to name a few, are emphatically pro-Castro. But Castro does not seem to have made a serious effort to set up a rigidly-controlled organization to compete with Moscow and Peking, although he did take the lead in establishing the Latin American Solidarity Organization (OLAS) as a revolutionary coordinating body.

The pro-Peking Communist parties in Latin America were formed by disaffected elements within the top echelons of the orthodox pro-Moscow parties who disagreed about the most effective strategy for gaining power. Frustrated by the cautious, peaceful path of socialism advocated by the old-line parties, these elements were attracted to a more militant strategy espoused by the Chinese Communists, which offered the prospect of an early access of power. They welcomed the Maoist doctrine of "people's war," and sought to capitalize on the Sino-Soviet rift by splitting away from the orthodox parties and setting up their own organizations.[55] The new pro-Peking parties drew much of their rank-and-file support from the "younger elements and youth organizations of the pro-Moscow parties, similarly disillusioned by the nonmilitant conservatism of the old-line leadership."[56]

By the end of the 1960s, there were pro-Peking parties in Argentina, Bolivia, Brazil, Chile, Colombia, the Dominican Republic, Ecuador, Mexico, Paraguay, Peru, and Puerto Rico. Like the Fidelista parties, the pro-Peking factions constitute a small and insignificant segment of the radical Left in Latin America. They lack the strength and cohesion of their pro-Moscow competitors.

Soviet Support for Latin American Communism

In the emerging era of detente, the Soviet Union has not renounced its competition for power and influence in Latin America and other parts of the Third World. Moscow continues to use every means at its disposal, including the loyal Communist parties, to create revolutionary situations everywhere throughout the non-Communist world. The growing trend toward East-West detente and superpower accommodation requires an intensification of ideological and class struggle.[57]

In the early 1970s, Moscow considered Latin America as the area of the Third World with the greatest "revolutionary potential." The revolutionary movement was believed to have entered an entirely new, more promising stage that offered fresh opportunities for the Moscow-line parties to gain or share power. The main reason

[55]Alexander, "The Communist Parties of Latin America," *loc. cit.,* p. 41.
[56]*Ibid.*
[57]See Boris Ponomarev, "Topical Problems in the Theory of World Revolutionary Powers," *Kommunist* (Moscow), no. 15 (October 1971). Ponomarev is Secretary of the Central Committee of the CPSU and has been in charge of relations between the CPSU and the nongoverning Communist parties since 1955. Ponomarev's article is an authoritative statement of the views of the Soviet leadership.

for this favorable development was the election of Salvador Allende's Communist-Socialist coalition government in Chile. The victory of the "Popular Unity bloc" was said to be of "tremendous general theoretical value." It vindicated the Soviet doctrines of the possibility of a peaceful acquisition of power, the leading role of the working class, the vital importance of a united front of leftist forces, the gradual takeover of the government by the Communists, and the importance of Soviet support as a protective shield against foreign and domestic counterrevolutionary activities. This optimistic assessment will no doubt be revised in the light of the violent overthrow of the Allende regime by the Chilean armed forces.

The extent to which an expanded Soviet presence in the area would bolster the sagging fortunes of the Communist movements, or enhance the tarnished image of communism as the "wave of the future," is open to question. Massive Soviet military and economic aid to Cuba has demonstrated that a Communist regime hostile to the United States can survive even in the Caribbean. But Cuba's client status and near-total dependence on the Soviet Union, the dismal economic performance of the Cuban "Socialist" experiment, and the failure of its sponsorship of armed struggle abroad have clearly weakened the appeal of Fidelista strategy for both the Communist and non-Communist Left.

Prospects for any of these rival Communist parties to gain or share power in Latin America are generally poor, and perhaps more so since the collapse of the Allende regime in September 1973. The best hope of the pro-Moscow and independent parties in the long run still lies in forming alliances with more popular left-wing nationalist groups and governments. The appearance of left-wing military or populist-oriented civilian governments may offer new opportunities to the Communists, and particularly the pro-Moscow parties. On the other hand, the economic nationalism and Socialist orientation of military and civilian populist regimes might well lessen the appeals of communism, especially to middle class students, intellectuals, and professionals, and thus place Moscow-line parties at a disadvantage in the struggle for decisive political power. Not only do they no longer monopolize the radical program; they must also face the fact that far more rapid and sweeping changes are advocated by their impatient, ultraleftist rivals.

7

Relations with Cuba:
Conflict and Accommodation

The involvement of Moscow and Havana in the Latin American revolutionary process has been marked by alternating periods of competition and cooperation resulting from differences in national interests, perceptions of Latin America's revolutionary prospects, and the respective bargaining power of both countries. But from the very beginning, both countries have shared certain common interests: weakening the position of the United States; the spread of Communist ideology; strengthening the Latin American revolutionary movement; and building communism in Cuba.

Immediately after Castro seized power, Cuban-organized guerrilla forces invaded the Dominican Republic, Haiti, Nicaragua, and Panama. All of these expeditions ended in complete disaster. There is no evidence that the Soviet Union was involved in any of Castro's early, romantic revolutionary misadventures. Moscow did agree, however, to help organize an effective intelligence service for Fidel Castro, including training in intelligence, subversion, and guerrilla operations. By the middle of 1961, the USSR had organized the DGI for clandestine operations overseas, and by the end of the year, Castro's agents were already infiltrating the Latin American countries.

Despite Castro's extraordinary success in Cuba, Moscow remained skeptical about revolutionary prospects in other Latin American countries. The Soviet leadership was also cautious about lending support to Castro, whom they viewed as an unpredictable Caribbean *caudillo* and revolutionary adventurer. They feared that Castro might embroil the Soviet Union in unwise revolutionary ventures, or in a dangerous confrontation with the United States in a region where the Americans enjoyed overwhelming military strength. Nevertheless, Moscow soon began to see some advantages in helping Castro organize more effectively for intelligence and foreign revolutionary activities.

Second Declaration of Havana

In February 1962, shortly after establishment of the Cuban DGI, Castro launched a new call (the socalled Second Declaration of Havana), and pledged Cuban support for the "liberation" of the continent. Five years of revolutionary activism followed. Havana provided arms, training, money, and sometimes leadership for the revolutionary movements in many Latin American countries. This period was marked by recurrent strain and tension between Cuba and the Soviet Union. The Soviet leadership was skeptical of Castro's ability to export revolution, and argued that the correct path — peaceful or nonpeaceful — should be decided by each country itself. Castro, on the other hand, believed that revolutionary violence could create revolutionary conditions. He was impatient of the longer, peaceful path to power. In the Second Declaration of Havana, Castro declined to mention "peaceful coexistence" or other Soviet-approved ideological formulas, and declared that guerrilla warfare was the only solution to the ills of the Third World.

Castro and Che Guevara, the two prophets of violent revolution, were clearly disappointed in the feeble response to their call to arms. In January 1963, Castro expressed his bitterness at the timidity of the Latin American revolutionaries, and the rejection of his policy by the nonviolent orthodox Communist parties of Latin

America. The Soviet leadership privately opposed his program on the ground that it did not conform to the teachings of Marxism-Leninism. It reflected left-wing adventurism of the most flagrant kind, and, worst of all, was bound to fail. During the 1960s, the USSR was regularly subjected to vitriolic attacks by Peking for "revisionism," and by the ultraleft in Latin America for having abandoned the revolution. In view of Russia's pretensions as the homeland of world revolution, this was a charge that could not be dismissed out of hand. To protect their left flank, the Russians continued to employ the rhetoric of the armed struggle, and gave some verbal support to the Castro line from time to time. Radio broadcasts and propaganda calling for armed revolt of the Andean Indians and other oppressed groups were stepped up. Limited support in the form of arms and money was also given to a few of the orthodox Communist parties (for example, in Venezuela and the Dominican Republic) that adopted the armed path to power.

Havana Conference

A secret meeting of 22 Latin American Communist parties was held in Havana in November 1964. Pro-Peking and ultraleftist factions were pointedly excluded. The meeting was called by the Soviet Union with the agreement of Castro and the established Latin American parties. Moscow's apparent objectives were to alienate Castro from Peking-oriented factions, and in general to isolate Latin American communism from Peking influence. It was an important event in the evolution of Cuban relations with the orthodox Moscow-line parties, since it brought Castro together for the first time with the leaders of the established parties from all over the continent.

At the meeting, Moscow and the Latin American Communists showed a willingness to make concessions to Castro's views on revolutionary strategy. In their dispute with Peking, the Soviet leaders had never adopted the position that the peaceful, electoral path to power was the only feasible strategy in all circumstances. Moscow had always insisted that both violent and nonviolent paths were possible, depending on circumstances in each country. Prior to the Havana conference, however, Moscow had stressed the peaceful path and played down the armed struggle. In Havana, the USSR, Cuba, and the Latin American parties adopted a resolution calling for "support in an active form to those who at present are subject to severe repression, such as the Venezuelan, Colombian, Honduran, Paraguyan, and Haitian fighters." Moscow's endorsement of the armed struggle in these six countries represented an important policy shift that no doubt pleased Castro and made it difficult for him to refuse further cooperation. For his part, Castro sided with Moscow in the Sino-Soviet dispute, after some initial reluctance.

By adopting a policy that placed greater emphasis on armed violence and accepted a diversity of positions, Moscow was able to restore a measure of unity among the Latin American parties. In the circumstances, there was little else that Moscow could do. The rise of guerrilla movements in the region, emboldened by Castro's success in Cuba, confronted Moscow and the pro-Moscow parties with a serious dilemma. In order to maintain its influence over the Latin American parties and exert some influence over the guerrillas, Moscow was forced to strike an uneasy balance between support for the more cautious orthodox parties, and the younger, impatient guerrilla leaders favoring the armed struggle.

The conference communique indicated that Moscow had agreed to support guerrilla warfare in exchange for Castro's agreement to deal only with the orthodox, Moscow-line parties in Latin America. Moreover, local Communist parties were expected to extend their support to Fidelista insurgencies only in the six countries named, while elsewhere the established parties could continue their customary opportunism, freed from the threat of Cuban-supported insurgencies on their left flank. The Havana conference resulted in a major schism between Havana and Peking, and initiated a brief period of Soviet-Cuban cooperation.

Tri-Continental Conference

The Tri-Continental Conference was less a meeting of

pro-Moscow Communist Party leaders than an assembly of less easily defined "popular" organizations from Asia, Africa, and Latin America sponsored by the Afro-Asian Peoples Solidarity Organization (AAPSO), with headquarters in Cairo. The Conference was planned and largely financed by the USSR as a means of using Castro against Peking in the arena of Third World radical international politics. Moscow hoped to create a new worldwide movement to replace AAPSO, which was weakened by the Sino-Soviet rivalry. Moscow's aim was to expand AAPSO (adding the pro-Moscow parties of Latin America to the anti-Peking forces already within AAPSO) so as to weaken Peking's claim to leadership of the Third World. Castro's role in the Soviet scheme was to insure that the Latin American representation at the Tri-Continental Conference would be dominated by the pro-Moscow Communist parties.

Castro used the Conference to assert himself as another Third World leader of the stature of Nasser or Nkrumah, who had previously hosted AAPSO sessions, and to recover some of the prestige lost after the humiliation of the 1962 missile crisis. While the Conference did not turn out entirely to Moscow's liking, both Castro and Moscow gained something of what they wanted from the other. The Russian delegate, Sharaf Rashidov, endorsed the Fidelista armed struggle in Latin America. Castro reciprocated by lashing out violently against China and abandoning his neutral stance in the Sino-Soviet conflict. This was a great victory for the USSR. Moscow's feeble disclaimer that the Soviet delegate's speech at the Conference did not reflect official policy was not taken seriously in Latin America. The interventionist implications of the Conference jeopardized Moscow's assiduously cultivated image as a peaceful diplomatic partner and led to strong protests by Latin American governments in the OAS and United Nations.

Latin American Solidarity Organization

Following his success in gaining support for the armed revolutionary struggle at the Tri-Continental Conference, Castro abandoned his aloofness from the Sino-Soviet dispute and became more actively involved in international Communist politics. He immediately formed a regional counterpart to AAPSO, called the Latin American Solidarity Organization (OLAS). The permanent steering committee, with headquarters in Havana, included representatives of the most important pro-Moscow Communist parties in Latin America. OLAS organized a Latin American Solidarity Conference in July-August 1967, which was attended by about 160 delegates from Latin America. The OLAS Conference was anti-Soviet in tone, and clearly showed the strained relationship still existing between Castro, on the one hand, and Moscow and the pro-Soviet Communist parties.

At this meeting, Castro bitterly denounced the Soviet Union and Soviet bloc countries for their lack of revolutionary zeal, and criticized their efforts to establish relations with "reactionary" Latin American governments. The conference endorsed Castro's revolutionary line, and militantly reaffirmed the armed struggle as the primary path for Latin America. Revolutionary war was to be waged with or without the support of the established Communist parties; and the role of revolutionary vanguard could be assigned to any group taking up the revolutionary struggle, not just to the Communists. By establishing a permanent OLAS committee in Havana to coordinate and provide material support to guerrilla movements, Castro openly defied Moscow's more pragmatic and opportunistic strategy in Latin America.

Throughout the mid-1960s, Moscow found itself in the embarrassing position of financing Castro's revolutionary ventures while having no control over them. Without massive Soviet economic and military aid, the Castro regime might well have collapsed. Russian state interests lay in establishing normal diplomatic relations with the Latin American countries and promoting popular front coalitions in the hope that the pro-Moscow parties would eventually come to power. But Soviet Communist Party interests were somewhat different. They called for the restoration of the unity of the world Communist movement under Soviet control, and to avoid being outflanked on the left by Peking and Havana.

Tightening the Screw

Castro failed to revitalize the guerrilla movement, however, and nothing symbolized his failure more dramatically than the death of Che Guevara in Bolivia in October 1967. From the outset, the Russians were skeptical of Guevara's Bolivian expedition, which was armed, trained, and financed by Castro, on practical grounds; but they nonetheless provided some support for it, as did the Czechs and East Germans. Guevara's disastrous end confirmed Moscow's worst predictions; and in private conversations with East European Communists, the Russians upbraided Castro for his rashness, stupidity, and infantile adventurism.

Stunned by Guevara's death, Castro was forced to reassess his obviously mistaken views of the revolutionary situation in Latin America. He abandoned the illusion that an effective revolutionary movement could be rebuilt in Latin America with himself as *líder máximo* The armed struggle was not succeeding and could not serve as a battering ram to break out of hemispheric isolation and enhance his leverage with Moscow. Castro was reluctantly compelled by circumstances—mainly Soviet economic pressures, serious economic problems at home, and the failure of revolution abroad—into a posture of revolutionary retrenchment in Latin America, while turning inward to focus on Cuba's domestic problems.

Relations between the USSR and Cuba reached their lowest point in late 1967 and early 1968. This was due, in large part, to Moscow's failure to retaliate against American bombing of North Vietnam. Membership in the Socialist camp evidently afforded little protection against American military action, except in Eastern Europe. The strained relations and bitter mutual recriminations were observable in the Escalante affair,[58] Cuba's boycott

---

[58]The old-line Communist, Anibal Escalante, ex-Executive Secretary of the defunct pro-Soviet Popular Socialist Party (PSP), and 34 other ex-members of the PSP were tried and sentenced in January 1968 for operating a socalled "microfaction" to oppose Castro's economic and foreign policies and urge his replacement by trustworthy old-line Communists.

of the Moscow-sponsored meeting of Communist parties in Bucharest, and the slowdown in Soviet economic aid in early 1968.

In view of all this, Castro's speech of August 23, 1968, in support of Moscow's right to invade Czechoslovakia, took Castro's supporters by surprise. By endorsing the Soviet operation against Czechoslovakia, Castro was defending what all Latin American countries rejected: great power intervention in the affairs of a small country. Castro's unexpected *volte-face* actually was dictated by self-interest. The Brezhnev Doctrine, which acknowledged Moscow's duty to intervene if a Socialist state was threatened, also promised greater security for the Castro regime. That this was no empty promise, as far as Cuba was concerned, was demonstrated by a series of Soviet naval visits beginning in July 1969. From Castro's viewpoint, the Soviet security guarantee, for which he had been pressing since 1969, was at last in sight.[59]

Intense economic pressure was also applied by Moscow in early 1968 to bring Castro into line. Unfortunately for Castro, his irrational and erratic "personalist" management of the Cuban economy (which led to a decline in *per capita* GNP of 0.6 percent per annum in the 1960s) had greatly strengthened Moscow's economic leverage in Havana.[60] The Russians not only threatened to cut off economic aid and oil shipments if Castro resisted their demands, but showed that they meant business by reducing the flow of oil to a trickle and halting the shipment of industrial raw materials. The East European countries followed suit. As the Cuban economy began to falter, Castro was forced to capitulate. His reward was the signing of new economic and military aid agreements.

Castro's speech on Czechoslovakia was a signal that the process of Cuban submission to Soviet interests had begun. Castro must have decided that he had no choice but to align himself more closely with Moscow. From his point of view, a break would have been a

[59]See Ernst Halperin, "Soviet Naval Power, Soviet-Cuban Relations, and Politics in the Caribbean," in James D. Theberge, ed., *Soviet Seapower in the Caribbean, Political and Strategic Implications* (New York: Praeger, 1972), p. 89.

[60]*World Bank Atlas.* (Washington: International Bank for Reconstruction and Development, 1972).

major calamity. It would have made him dependent on the Western powers, from which he was unlikely to get the necessary support for his economic projects and revolutionary ambitions. The decision to accept the leadership of Moscow was obviously not an easy one. It had been Castro's great ambition to restore real independence to Cuba; and for a while in the early and mid-1960s, he appeared to have succeeded. His mistake was to attempt to accomplish too much with the meager resources at his command: industrialization and social revolution, a leading role in the Third World, revolutionary campaigns in Latin America, and the "liberation" of the continent from American influence.

Instead, Castro found that, as a result of his bitter hatred of the United States, he had maneuvered himself into a position of almost complete dependence on the Soviet Union. Cuba needed arms and economic aid for which it could not pay. There was no prospect of receiving aircraft, naval vessels, and military equipment free of charge from anyone but Russia. Nobody except Russia would continue to make loans to Cuba year after year with little prospect of repayment. Castro was, of course, aware of his weakened bargaining position *vis-à-vis* Moscow. But he had no alternative. He made concession after concession to the Russians, purging the intelligence service of cadres considered undesirable in Moscow, cooperating with the traditional pro-Moscow parties, refraining from criticism of the Soviet Union, cutting back on his support for revolutionary violence, rationalizing economic management, and supporting Moscow's policies in the United Nations and throughout the Third World. Castro found it increasingly difficult to square these concessions with what used to be his fierce attachment to Cuban sovereignty and independence.

As for Moscow, the domestication of Castro opened up new possibilities for closer cooperation between Cuba and the Soviet Union in Latin America and the Third World. Moscow seems to have decided that its best interests were served by ending the permanent emergency situation in Cuba and bringing about the normalization of Cuba's relations with its Hemispheric neighbors—above all,

Venezuela and the United States. Cuba would be able to break out of its diplomatic and commercial isolation only by eschewing revolutionary violence (although not necessarily its revolutionary rhetoric).

Castro's new foreign policy orientation was evident in Havana's diplomatic offensive in Latin America in the early 1970s, which embraced not only progressive, "anti-imperialist" regimes, like Allende's Chile and Velasco's Peru, but also friends of the United States such as Trinidad and Barbados. On various occasions since the end of 1971, Cuban officials have expressed an interest in normalizing relations with the United States on the condition that Washington was willing to abandon its trade embargo. For its part, Moscow privately encouraged both Cuba and the United States to work out a settlement of their differences and to resume diplomatic and commercial relations.

The resumption of Cuban-American trade clearly would provide greater benefits to Cuba and the USSR than to the United States, particularly if Washington failed to demand a *quid pro quo* from Havana. Cuba would be able to earn dollars for exports to the US market, obtain access to US commercial credits, and purchase needed American machinery and spare parts (now obtained through third parties) at lower prices. Russia's economic subsidy of the Castro regime would be substantially reduced. In the Soviet scheme of things, Cuban trade with the United States would eventually earn the hard currency needed to finance oil imports from Venezuela, Cuba's major supplier before Castro came to power. This would relieve Moscow of the burden of the rising cost of supplying Cuba with oil and subsidizing the Cuban economy at the present rate of about $1 billion a year.

Castro continues to rely on revolutionary rhetoric to propagate the myth that he is the leader of the "second national liberation movement" in Latin America. But the reality is now different. In the emerging era of superpower detente, Castro finds himself in a weak and uncomfortable situation. Dependent on the Soviet Union for survival, he is no longer feared and the Cuban revolution fails to inspire imitation. As long as Cuba remains so critically dependent on Moscow for economic and military aid, Castro's foreign policy must necessarily follow the leadership of the Soviet Union: peaceful coexistence abroad, even with the United States, and Soviet-style economic reconstruction at home.

8

The Soviet Naval Presence in Caribbean Waters

During the last half century, the Soviet Navy's primary mission has been the defense of the homeland against attack from the sea. In the first decade after World War II, the principal maritime threat was perceived by Moscow to be a seaborne invasion launched by the West. But as the United States acquired a seaborne strategic strike capability, the Soviet Union reordered its priorities; and Soviet naval policy thereafter gave paramount attention to the task of countering the Western strike force. Moscow invested heavily in the development of naval nuclear technology, and built up a large, modern fleet of warships and auxiliaries that expanded Soviet capabilities for long-range operations.

By the early 1960s, Moscow had adopted a policy of forward naval deployment in order to balance the range of the US carrier strike force and Polaris submarines. It was not long before Soviet surface units around the world began to serve political as well as strategic purposes. In the Mediterranean, the primary mission of the Soviet naval force is strategic defense, but Moscow also stressed its political mission of neutralizing Western capabilities (mainly the US Sixth Fleet) against its Arab clients. The Soviet

Union was, in fact, successful in deterring Israeli air strikes against Port Said and Alexandria by establishing a permanent naval presence in those Egyptian ports. On more distant seas — the Gulf of Guinea, the Caribbean, and the Indian Ocean — Soviet naval units were used politically in various ways: in 1968, to pressure Ghana to release two impounded Soviet fishing vessels by a display of naval force in the Gulf of Guinea; in 1969-70, to probe US reaction to a forward submarine base in Cuba; in 1970, to intervene in support of Somalia's military government by means of a naval visit that lasted until an allegedly revolutionary plot was defeated; and in the same year, to prevent a recurrence of a Portuguese-supported attack on Conakry, Guinea, by establishing a regular patrol off the Guinea coast. The increased numbers, mobility, and readiness of Soviet naval forces in distant waters will undoubtedly permit future operations in support of foreign policy objectives that lie outside the primary naval tasks of strategic defense and mutual deterrence.

Caribbean Naval Presence

The appearance of a seven-ship Soviet naval squadron in the Caribbean and Gulf of Mexico in early July 1969 signalled a new chapter in the political evolution of the Western Hemisphere. For the first time since the destruction of the Spanish fleet off Santiago de Cuba in July 3, 1898, the naval force of a rival great power entered the Caribbean. Through April 1974, Soviet warships made 12 visits to Cuba: once in 1969 (July); three times in 1970 (May, September, and December); three times in 1971 (February, May, and November); three times in 1972 (March, May, and November); once in 1973 (August); and at least once in 1974 (April). The Soviet naval squadrons were divided about equally between surface vessels and submarines (both diesel and nuclear-powered) with tenders.

The Soviet naval intrusion into the Caribbean obviously cannot be explained in terms of "natural" Russian interests such as might apply to waters adjacent to the Russian homeland. The Caribbean is not by any stretch of the definition an area of "vital" security interest to Moscow, notwithstanding the fact that the preservation of "Socialist" Cuba is clearly a high priority objective. The Soviets have not maintained longstanding political and economic relationships with countries of the area; and moreover, a Soviet naval deployment in the Caribbean is extremely vulnerable to American power.

Nevertheless, Soviet warships are now active in Caribbean waters. There appear to be a number of reasons for this. The unprecedented Soviet naval construction program in the 1960s created a naval capability available for flag-showing missions all over the world that emphasized Russia's coming of age as a superpower with global interests. The existence of an accessible "Socialist" client state provided a convenient justification for naval visits and winter training cruises in warm waters. Moreover, the Soviet Union is still striving to expand its influence into such areas as the Caribbean and South America, from which it had hitherto been excluded.

Submarine Base at Cienfuegos

During the Summer and Fall of 1970, the USSR built a nuclear submarine support facility at Cienfuegos on the southern coast of Cuba. The incident provoked a minor crisis in US-Soviet relations. After some initial hesitancy, Washington warned Moscow against any attempt to make the base operational by servicing Soviet strategic submarines "in or from" Cuba. The crisis was brought to a close in October 1970, when the USSR agreed to abide by the 1962 Kennedy-Khrushchev understanding that ended the missile crisis and prohibited the USSR from introducing offensive weapons systems into the Western Hemisphere. The Nixon Administration apparently reached a secret agreement with the USSR that the servicing of submarines in Cuba would contravene the 1962 ban on offensive weapons.

Soviet naval activities after the Cienfuegos crisis suggested that the Soviet Union is seeking to maintain some form of continuous naval presence in the Caribbean. This presence could take two forms. One is a capability to support missile-carrying submarines in the western Atlantic by means of a submarine tender operating in the area. The other possibility would be frequent visits to Cuba by Soviet surface naval vessels that could conceivably lead to permanent stationing in Cuba. Moscow's gradual upgrading of its naval presence in the Caribbean apparently is intended to assert its rights as a global naval power, to test US reactions, and to familiarize the United States and the Caribbean states with the face of a Soviet naval presence. Both forms of naval presence are of greater potential political than military significance.

US-Soviet "understandings" appear to limit only one aspect of Soviet naval power in the Caribbean, albeit an important one—namely, the use of Cuban bases by missile-carrying submarines or their servicing from tenders based in Cuba. It apparently does not cover surface support of strategic submarines in Caribbean waters by vessels not based in Cuba, or the operations of nuclear-armed surface ships. Subsequent TU-95 flights to Cuba, and Cuba-based surveillance flights off the US east coast in November 1972, served to emphasize Moscow's right to maintain a military presence in the area. This may explain why, unlike 1962, Castro failed to protest the 1970 US-Soviet understanding.

At present, Moscow has a fully prepared forward anchorage in Cuba that could be activated at any time by the arrival of a submarine tender. The Soviet Navy has also demonstrated its ability to service submarines on the high seas. The necessary tenders could be supported from the logistics base at Cienfuegos or some other port. Thus supported, Soviet submarines would be able to operate within range of more than half the United States during their patrol period, including transit time to and from Cienfuegos. Furthermore, the Russians would be able to double the on-station time for their Y-class strategic submarines.

The Soviet attempt to establish a base at Cienfuegos is consistent with recent Soviet efforts to acquire similar facilities in other parts of the world. These initiatives are apparently aimed at enhancing the flexibility of Soviet naval power, especially by giving it the capability to maintain a continuous presence and conduct operations at great distances from the Soviet Union.

Political Uses of Naval Power

Gunboat diplomacy has traditionally been aimed at exercising political influence over client states or colonies and protecting them from interference by rival powers. In the case of the European empires, some kind of administrative structure existed ashore, supported by naval force. Circumstances have undoubtedly changed since the passing of the imperial era. Nowadays, great powers tend to acquire costly and ungrateful clients rather than pliant and sometimes profitable colonies. Yet, today as in the past, warships continue to be used in peacetime, in one form or another, to supplement diplomacy and support political objectives in distant waters.

In the Caribbean, the employment of Soviet naval power for such purposes runs the risk of military confrontation with the United States. Normally, the Soviet Union is far too cautious to court such risks in an area recognized as being within a US security zone and where the United States enjoys overwhelming naval predominance. But opportunities may well present themselves for using Soviet naval power for political advantage in the Caribbean and South American waters. Soviet naval operations in the Caribbean have already served to bolster the sagging morale of the Cuban regime and reassure Havana of Moscow's determination to protect its client. On the other hand, Castro is no doubt aware of the Soviet Union's failure to support other client states such as Egypt in time of need when that course conflicted with broader Soviet interests.

By sending warships into the Caribbean on a regular basis, Moscow has also acquired potential leverage for forcing the withdrawal of US forward naval deployments from waters close to the Soviet Union. Moscow has made regular overtures to the West aimed at removing or limiting the operations of Western forces in the Mediterranean and Indian Ocean under the guise of denuclearization, creation of zones of peace, or mutual withdrawal of naval forces. In June 1971, for example, Brezhnev stated that the Soviet Union would be prepared to negotiate an agreement limiting Soviet and Western naval deployments to the Mediterranean, the Indian Ocean, and "other seas."[61]

While Moscow has not publicly raised the question of American withdrawal from its base in Guantanamo in exchange for limitations on Soviet naval visits to Cuba, there is evidence that Moscow would be prepared to discuss such a trade-off since the balance of advantage is so clearly on the Soviet side.[62] Unless it formed part of a farreaching settlement between Washington and Havana, the abandonment of Guantanamo would be a striking gain for Castro and a severe blow to the ability of the United States to maintain military facilities elsewhere in the Caribbean. In any event, Moscow is aware that its naval visits and military presence in Cuba constitute valuable bargaining counters in future negotiations with the United States.

Under certain circumstances, the Soviets might be able to derive some political advantage in the Caribbean and South America from strengthening its military presence in the region. The Russians continuously strive to strengthen the leftward currents of Latin American politics; and the message propagated by Moscow is that national liberation movements and anti-imperialist forces in the Third World countries can succeed only in close cooperation with the Soviet bloc. A stronger Soviet naval presence in the Hemisphere could lend greater credibility to this claim.

Furthermore, the potential of a Soviet naval presence is not limited merely to "showing the flag" or swaying local attitudes. The possible use of force is never completely absent from Soviet

[61]*Pravda*, June 12, 1971.

[62]See the report of an interview with Russian diplomats in Havana in the *Boston Herald and Traveler*, September 10, 1972.

calculations, particularly in countries like Haiti, where the united front strategy does not apply. In the event of local upheavals, the presence of Soviet surface warships in the area might well inhibit US intervention, as they now do in the Middle East. In the case of internal challenges to the Cuban government, a Soviet naval presence could also neutralize certain elements of the opposition.

It is important, however, not to exaggerate these dangers. The changing character of the US-Soviet relationship is more likely to encourage prudence and restraint in Latin America than adventurism. But there is still a considerable uncertainty as to the outcome of this new relationship. The next several years will determine whether competition between the two superpowers will take on an essentially cooperative or hostile character. Meanwhile, the potential long-term risks posed by the increased visibility of a rival military power in Latin America should not be lightly dismissed.

9

Key Targets of Soviet Diplomacy: Chile and Peru

In 1935, Moscow dispatched Eudocio Ravines, a brilliant Peruvian Communist organizer, to Chile to implement the "united front" and "antifascist popular front" strategy that had replaced the ultraleft strategy of the Comintern. Since that time, the Chilean Communist Party has generally followed a strategy of broad alliance and limited aims. One of the most loyal pro-Soviet parties in Latin America, it gave unqualified support to the Soviet bloc invasion of Czechoslovakia in 1968. While the fortunes of the Party have varied through the years as a result of domestic and international developments, it unstintingly supported the twists and turns of Soviet foreign policy and repeated Moscow's themes of anti-imperialism and class warfare.

The Chilean Communist Party, at least prior to the September 1973 military coup, was the best organized and strongest Party in Latin America. Between 1956 and 1969, it formed an uneasy electoral alliance with the Socialist Party of Chile, its more militant Marxist rival on the Left. But in 1969, the Communists decided that a much more broadly-based alliance of left-wing forces was necessary in order to transform Chile into a Socialist state. The Communists thus played a key role in the founding of the Popular

Unity Front (a coalition of six leftist parties) at the end of 1969. After the 1970 electoral victory of the Popular Unity Front under Salvador Allende, the Communists became the single most influential force within the coalition. It was a far better organized and disciplined participant than its closest rival, the ideologically more unstable and militant Socialist Party.

The ultimate aim of the Chilean Communist Party did not waver throughout the Allende period. It was to take advantage of the weaknesses of Chile's democratic institutions and to install a "dictatorship of the proletariat" under Communist Party direction.[63] The strategy, which was shared by Allende and the "moderate" wing of the Socialist Party, was to "overthrow" the bourgeois state and constitution by means of the legal device of the plebiscite.[64] Mass mobilization, the infiltration of Chilean institutions, and tactical alliances with the opposition were to be employed to generate sufficient popular support. Congress was to be replaced by a "popular assembly," and the existing legal system by "popular tribunals." President Allende's pledge to uphold the Statute of Guarantees (designed to commit his government to preserve Chile's democratic freedoms and institutions in exchange for Congressional support) was simply a "tactical necessity" to gain power, as he explained later.[65]

The *via Chilena* proclaimed by Allende soon after his election was widely misunderstood in the West. The image officially propagated at home and abroad was of a uniquely Chilean path to a new type of Marxist-humanist socialism, where basic liberties, economic pluralism, and free elections were respected by all. Western

---

[63] See Eduardo Labarca, *Corvalan 27 Horas* (Santiago: Editorial Quimantu, 1972), p.110. Luis Corvalan, Secretary General of the Chilean Communist Party, declared: "For us (Communists), the path from capitalism to socialism necessarily requires that the proletariat be converted into the leading class, into the determining social force."

[64] In an interview with Regis Debray in 1971, Salvador Allende said: "As for the bourgeois state at the present moment, we are seeking to overcome it. To overthrow it." Regis Debray, *The Chilean Revolution, Conversations with Allende* (New York: Random House, 1971), p. 82.

[65] *Ibid.*, p. 119.

liberals were misled to believe that the Allende government was constructing a new West European type of democratic socialism in Chile. This image clashed with the realities of Allende's revolutionary ambition.

The Chilean Communists and their allies in Moscow were themselves uneasy about the ideological implications of the *via Chilena* advocated by Salvador Allende,[66] and refused to endorse it as a uniquely Chilean path to socialism since it implied that the Communists might not necessarily assume the leading role after the Popular Unity coalition achieved total power. The Chilean Party supported Moscow's doctrine of *via pacifica*, which accepted free elections and popular pluralism as a short-term tactical device under Chilean conditions, but aimed in the long run at installing a Soviet-style Communist dictatorship. This *via pacífica* was not as "pacific" as the slogan implied. It embraced all forms of class conflict and violence short of armed insurrection and civil war in the process of establishing the dictatorship of the proletariat.

Allende's foreign policy was very much to Moscow's liking. It featured the doctrine of "ideological pluralism" (relations with all states regardless of ideology and internal political character), closer relations with the Socialist camp, seizure of US investments, and encouragement of an "anti-imperialist" front in Latin America. Under the Allende regime, previously close ties with the United States were replaced by strong political and economic relationships with the "Socialist countries," above all, Cuba and the USSR. The first trip of the Chilean Foreign Minister, Clodomiro Almeyda, outside of Latin America was to the USSR and Eastern Europe, in May-June 1971. President Allende visited Moscow in December 1972. Strong ideological and personal ties linked the Chilean Communist Party with the Soviet Party leadership, and Salvador Allende with Fidel Castro.

---

[66]See Labarca, *op. cit.;* and Luis Corvalan, *Camino de Victoria*, (Santiago: 1971), pp. 32, 35, and 59-60, for authoritative statements of the Communist Party position.

President Allende's description of the USSR as Chile's "big brother" (*hermano mayor*) was no mere figure of speech; it reflected his expectation that the USSR would become the most important Socialist ally of the Chilean revolution and the main economic bulwark of the regime. Moscow did, in fact, become the principal source of economic assistance to the Popular Unity government. Of a total of $620 million ($156.5 million in short-term credit and $463.5 million in project aid and supplier credits) authorized by the Socialist countries in the 1971-73 period,[67] the USSR provided $260.5 million ($98.5 million in short-term credit and $162.0 million in economic aid), most of which was never utilized. This was far from the massive help Allende needed. But Moscow was under no illusion that its economic cooperation would decisively influence the immediate prospects for radical social and economic transformation, although it would no doubt help to reduce Chile's dependence on the United States.

Soviet influence in Chile expanded rapidly as a result of the Chilean Communist Party's loyalty to the USSR and the expansion of Soviet-Chilean economic, technical, scientific, and cultural cooperation. As time went on, Moscow became increasingly alarmed at the deterioration of the economic situation, the violent clashes between the ultraleft and the ultraright, and the growing organization and strength of opposition forces, particularly after the Popular Unity government failed in March 1973 to obtain the majority electoral support required to transform Chile's political and economic structure by peaceful, constitutional means.

Nevertheless, Moscow was not willing to provide the massive short-term commodity assistance (such as foodstuffs) or untied convertible currency credits which the Allende regime needed to finance the import of food, spare parts, and machinery necessary to alleviate local shortages. Moscow's $98.5 million in short-term bank credits were no doubt helpful, but fell far short of Chile's import requirements, which, for food alone, were running at the rate

[67]See *Deuda Externa de Chile*, (Santiago: Departamento de Creditos Externos, CORFO, 1973), vol. 5, for full details.

of about $700 million a year when the Allende regime collapsed. The
Soviet leadership told Chilean Communist and Popular Unity officials that the main effort to improve the economic situation would
have to be made by the Allende government.[68] Moscow repeatedly
stressed that the Popular Unity government must reverse the
calamitous decline in production and productivity in order to have a
chance of winning over a majority of the Chileans to the cause of
socialism. Unwilling to give Allende the hard currency credits he
needed to improve his worsening chances for survival, Moscow
contented itself with organizing solidarity meetings at home and
abroad in the hope that these demonstrations would "reach the ears
of the Chilean people."[69] In the final analysis, Moscow stood idly
by while the *via pacífica* was destroyed by the disastrous policies of
President Allende and his Popular Unity government.

Moscow in fact pursued a dual strategy in Chile. At the level of
state-to-state relations, the USSR acted cautiously, adopted a noninterventionist posture, and encouraged anti-Americanism and
independence from the United States. Since Moscow realized that
the internal balance of forces did not favor the armed struggle, the
Popular Unity leadership was urged to maintain internal unity,
reject the "provocative and adventurous" overtures of the
ultraleft, avoid actions that might provoke a civil war, adopt a more
rational economic policy, and consolidate the gains of the revolution. At the same time, Moscow did nothing to restrain direct
Cuban involvement in the Chilean revolution. Protected by a
friendly, Marxist-dominated government and its Marxist President, Cuba transported large quantities of Soviet and Czechoslovak weapons to the radical left in Chile on Cuban planes and mer-
chant ships. Cuba also established a guerrilla training base and
coordinating center in Chile. The large intelligence team in the
Cuban Embassy in Santiago maintained liaison with the liberation
movement in Argentina, Bolivia, and Uruguay. DGI, Cuba's
Soviet-controlled intelligence service, also had close ties with the

[68]This "self-help" theme was repeated frequently by the Chilean Communist Party
    leadership when referring to Soviet assistance.
[69]*Radio Moscow* (in Spanish), August 19, 1973.

Chilean ultraleftist and other revolutionary exile groups, providing them with training, arms, and funds for the armed struggle in Chile and other Latin American countries.

Soviet army personnel were also directly involved in the training of worker-revolutionaries for urban guerrilla warfare. This occurred during 1972-73 at El Belloto, near Valparaiso, where the USSR had installed a factory for the manufacture of prefabricated housing for the Allende government. The firm (KPD) employed 20 Russians, eight of whom were engineers and technicians, and the remaining 12 were Soviet Army officers. After working hours, the 12 officers instructed a hard core of specially-selected worker-revolutionaries in the use of arms, street fighting, and urban guerrilla tactics. The Russian-built factory was kept under constant surveillance by Chile's naval intelligence. On the morning of September 11, 1973, the latter arrested the 20 Russians and a few days later expelled them from the country.[70]

This clandestine involvement in training guerrillas in Chile was an exception to Moscow's official line of giving full support to the legal and peaceful path to socialism. But Russia operates on the principle that since every eventuality cannot be foreseen, it is better to take precautionary measures that "contradict" the official line than to be sorry later. In Chile, there clearly were advantages in having some armed revolutionaries under direct Soviet control. Moscow would thus be able to retain a measure of influence over the Chilean ultraleft in the event that it was successful in seizing power.

The Soviet Union made every effort to extract the maximum advantage from its technical assistance program in Chile. Moscow assigned 46 technicians to the nationalized copper industry, all of whom were engaged in industrial espionage. According to Chilean mining technicians, the Soviet specialists during their two-year stay in Chile contributed nothing to the improvement of mining operations and were mainly occupied in gathering information on

[70]*Ercilla* (Santiago), October 10-16, 1973; and author's interviews with the Chilean military, December 1973.

American mining equipment, techniques, organization, and costs and productivity.[71] Moscow was also interested in fisheries and fishery-related (oceanographic, hydrographic, and marine biological research) activities in Chile. Fisheries aid to Chile gave the Soviet Union access to Chilean ports for its fishing, oceanographic, and other vessels, accustomed the Chileans to a Soviet maritime presence, and established a Soviet presence in another maritime area. The growing Soviet maritime presence in Chilean waters, around the Cape, and in sub-Antarctic waters, also provided a cover for gathering intelligence and oceanographic data of use to the Soviet Navy.

The Soviet Union offered to supply $300 million in military equipment to Allende in 1971. Moscow hoped to establish an important precedent in supplying arms to non-Communist countries in Latin America and further weaken Washington's already strained relations with Latin American military leaders. But the Chilean military refused the offer and decided to continue to obtain arms from the United States and other Western suppliers.[72] The anti-Communist military leadership was disturbed by growing potential violence and the deepening economic crisis. They were anxious not to weaken ties with the United States and Western Europe by turning to the Soviet Union for arms. Despite the coolness of official US-Chilean relations, the United States continued to maintain friendly relations with the Chilean military throughout the Allende period.

Moscow was very much aware of the weakness of the Allende regime. Not only was it a minority government (in 1970, 36 percent, and in 1973, 43 percent of the electorate supported the Popular Unity coalition), but the armed forces and powerful National Police were strongly anti-Communist. Since the "democratic forces"

[71]Statement of Andres Zauschquevich, Executive Vice President of the Chilean Copper Corporation, to the author in December 1973.

[72]In October 1971, the Chilean government officially denied that there had been any negotiations or offers from the USSR concerning the supply of arms. *Latin* (Buenos Aires), October 19, 1971. According to the Chilean military high command, however, Moscow had made an offer of $300 million in arms.

lacked sufficient political and economic power, Moscow favored a gradual takeover by the Chilean Communists and avoidance of a military struggle at all costs. Both the ultraleftist and ultrarightist opponents of the Allende government were attacked regularly in the Soviet press. The Movement of the Revolutionary Left (MIR), an ultraleftist group that deliberately sought a violent confrontation with the opposition, was singled out for particularly scathing criticism. It was charged with "revolutionary adventurism," contributing to political instability, and damaging prospects for the survival of the Popular Unity government.

From mid-1972 onwards, Moscow realized that opposition to the Allende government was growing rapidly. It was only the shrewd personality of Allende—skilled in maintaining a balance between the disruptive forces within his own government—that held together the disintegrating fabric of Chilean society. There was continued sharp criticism of irrational economic management, declining agricultural and industrial production, accelerating inflation, and the worsening balance of payments. Soviet observers advised a slower takeover of the economy, nationalizing the large firms first but leaving the small and medium-sized firms alone for the time being. In the last months before the military coup, the Soviet Union saw the handwriting on the wall and urged a consolidation of economic gains already achieved, collaboration with the opposition political parties (especially the Christian Democrats), and—always—the avoidance of armed conflict.

Thus, Moscow was deeply disturbed but not especially surprised by Allende's downfall on September 11, 1973. Tass admitted that the "Chilean experience was bitter and dramatic,"[73] and Fidel Castro declared that he was "very upset by events in Chile."[74] Moscow severed diplomatic relations with Santiago because of alleged persecution of Soviet officials by the military junta. After less than a week in power, the new regime began to feel the full blast

[73]Tass, September 20, 1973.

[74]*Ibid.*, September 13, 1973. The junta immediately broke relations with Havana for flagrant meddling in Chile's internal affairs.

of Soviet displeasure and frustration, expressed in a sustained and well-orchestrated propaganda campaign aimed at isolating and discrediting the regime. Soviet media accused the junta of "persecuting left-wingers with unparalleled cruelty."[75] They reported that "the streets of Santiago were flowing with blood,"[76] and that "tens of thousands of Chilean democrats" had been killed.[77] President Allende was alternatively reported to have been "murdered in cold blood" or to have died a hero's death resisting the rebels to the very end. In retaliation, Allende's residence was alleged to have been "wiped off the face of the earth."[78] The junta was shooting at women and children in an attempt to intimidate the people.[79] Tass indignantly blamed the CIA, Chilean "reaction," and "American monopolies" for organizing the military coup.[80] Even Leonid Brezhnev, not known for his devotion to Western democracy, expressed horror at the "monstrous, completely open violation of a country's constitution, the unceremonious flouting of the democratic traditions of an entire nation."[81]

Overthrow of the Allende government was a setback for Moscow's united front tactics in Latin America and had adverse repercussions for Marxist parties elsewhere in the West. Communists and Socialists in France and Italy, who had earlier pointed to Chile as a model of the peaceful transition to socialism, moved to disengage themselves from the Allende disaster. Instead of leading to socialism, united front tactics in Chile ushered in a period of unparalleled political violence, enormous suffering for Chile's workers and middle class, and the worst economic crisis in Chilean history. Non-Communist political parties in Latin America and the armed forces were also reminded of the grave risks of entering into an alliance with totalitarian parties.

[75]Moscow Radio, September 18, 1973.
[76]*Pravda*, September 26, 1973.
[77]Moscow Radio, October 28, 1973.
[78]*Ibid.*, September 18, 1973.
[79]*Ibid.*, September 28, 973.
[80]Tass, October 29, 1973.
[81]Moscow Radio, October 26, 1973.

Peru's Revolutionary Generals

Moscow has also given special attention to Peru since the October 1968 military coup that overthrew the government of President Fernando Belaunde Terry. The new Peruvian military regime, headed by General Juan Velasco Alvarado, was militantly nationalistic and exhibited a strong anticapitalist and anti-American orientation. It proclaimed a neutralist or nonaligned foreign policy that professed to be equally opposed to capitalism and communism. Within a few years, Peru had established close political and economic ties with the Soviet Union and Cuba, not as a result of Communist "propaganda" or "infiltration," but as part of the process of internal radicalization.

There was a great deal of resentment against the United States in Peru at the time of the military takeover. US policies in the 1960s had created strong anti-American currents within the armed forces. Washington refused to sell supersonic aircraft to the Peruvian Air Force, while at the same time pressuring the Belaunde government not to purchase French Mirages. Little money was allocated to Peru under the Alliance for Progress; and in general, Washington adopted a cool attitude toward the military junta in 1968. The suspension of all military sales and economic aid as a result of a fisheries dispute and the seizure of the assets of the International Petroleum Company (IPC), only made matters worse. Many Peruvian officers and civilians felt a sense of betrayal by a traditionally friendly country.

Economic backwardness, domestic social problems, and the corruption and ineffectiveness of civilian politicians also contributed to the radicalization of the Peruvian military. Under the influence of military and civilian intellectuals at the Center for Higher Military Studies (CAEM), and the impact of the antiguerrilla campaign against the Movement of the Revolutionary Left (MIR) and the Army of National Liberation (ELN), the Peruvian military evolved its own doctrine linking national security and economic development. The existing economic and social structure came to be considered so inefficient and unjust that it seriously threatened national security and the continued existence of the military as an institution. Such conditions could be exploited not only by the Communists, but also by Peru's ruling oligarchy in alliance with US interests that allegedly favored Peruvian backwardness.

The Velasco regime immediately attracted the interest of the Soviet Union. The first act of the military government was to expropriate without compensation the $200 million La Brea oilfield and Talara refinery complex owned by the IPC, a subsidiary of Standard Oil of New Jersey. The Velasco regime claimed that IPC was a special case and did not signal wholesale seizure without compensation of foreign interests. But the trend since 1968 has been toward the piecemeal liquidation of foreign investments in mining, banking, manufacturing, communications, transportation, certain areas of commerce, and the fish-meal industry. The Velasco regime moved steadily ahead with its program of expropriation, but it was not accomplished without considerable economic cost to Peru. The outright confiscation of IPC and the government's refusal to pay more than a fraction of the value of other expropriated American properties seriously strained relations with Washington. In February 1974, the Peruvian military regime advanced a serious proposal to reach a settlement. It agreed to pay $76 million in compensation for the expropriated companies, and another $74 million in profits, dividends, and royalties.[82]

The Velasco government also undertook a series of measures designed radically to transform the economy. New laws and decrees established industrial and mining "communities"(guaranteeing worker participation in management and profits) in the socalled "reformed" private sector. The state sector was vastly expanded and strengthened, and new "social property" enterprises were authorized. Despite the government's claim to favor the coexistence of several forms of productive enterprise, the reform aims at the virtual elimination of private enterprise in Peru, the remnants of which are to be relegated to a small "pure" capitalist

[82]*New York Times*, February 20, 1974.

sector comprised of petty merchants, tradesmen, artisans, and other small enterprises.

It is open to question whether these measures were "Socialist" in character (as critics of the government alleged) or constituted a new and original "third way" between capitalism and communism (as Velasco claimed). From the Soviet point of view, the reforms were a step in the right direction, since they undermined the foundations of private ownership and moved Peru perceptibly away from the capitalist system. The official Soviet appraisal was that Peru was "striving to find its own road to noncapitalist development" and that, "once capitalism had been rejected," Peru would "choose the Socialist road."[83] The Peruvian Communist Party, which supports the military regime, viewed the "industrial community" as a "transitional stage that would lead to socialism in due course."[84] Whatever the final outcome, the assumption of control over large sectors of the economy by an emerging military-technical elite indicated a sharp internal turn to the left.

As a pragmatic exponent of "ideological pluralism" and non-alignment, the Velasco regime found it easy enough to accommodate itself to the Soviet Union, provided that Russian help was forthcoming. The Soviet Union was thought of as a powerful but distant country whose support against American pressures could be used to Peru's advantage. The staunchly anti-Communist Peruvian military was not afraid of Soviet domination or penetration. It needed Russia (and Cuba) to affirm its independent foreign policy line, and it had something to offer in return. Peru is a country rich in oil, fishery resources, and other raw materials in world demand, and it was also a better choice than Allende's Chile as a potential model of noncapitalist development and as a showcase of Soviet economic cooperation.

[83]V. Tikhmenev in *Mirovaya ekonomika i mezhdunarodnyve otnosheniya*, no. 3 (1971).

[84]See the statement of Jorge del Prado, General Secretary of the Peruvian Communist Party, in *World Marxist Review*, no. 1 (1971).

In the early 1970s, political and economic ties with Cuba and especially the Soviet Union became progressively closer, and the Peruvian military gave the impression of being more friendly toward the USSR than its traditional Western allies. In numerous statements in 1973 and 1974, President Velasco and other Army ministers strongly praised the Soviet Union and Cuba, while reserving their criticism for the Western powers and Western "capitalism," and particularly for the United States.[85] Reviewing five years of diplomatic relations with the USSR at the end of 1973, President Velasco declared that Peru's relations with the USSR were "very promising" and had become "closer at all levels."[86]

Economic relations with the USSR took an upturn under the Velasco regime; but, as in the case of Allende's Chile, did not measure up to the exaggerated propaganda put out by both countries. Peru had hoped to make up for the decline in capital inflows from the United States, the international lending agencies, and foreign investors, resulting from its own confiscatory and anticapitalist policies, by obtaining aid and credits from the Soviet Union and the Socialist camp. However, no large-scale Soviet economic assistance was forthcoming, much to the disappointment of the Peruvian government. During the first four years (1968-72) of the Velasco regime, Russia provided only $28 million in economic credits, while Eastern Europe supplied $173 million. Much of Soviet technical assistance has taken the form of survey and planning work for specific projects which presumably will lead to economic cooperation with Peru in the future. Moscow refused to finance the $350 million Olmos hydroelectric and irrigation project, and only agreed to a three-year $6 million feasibility study for the initial stage. After much publicity concerning Soviet financing for a major part of the $45 million fishing port complex at Paita, Moscow provided only $1.8 million in technical assistance, machinery and

[85]The anti-Western and anticapitalist bias in the statements of General Edgardo Mercado Jarrin, Prime Minister; General Jorge Fernandez Maldonado, Minister of Mines and Energy; and General Javier Tantalean Vanini, Minister of Fisheries, have been particularly pronounced in recent years.

[86]News conference of President Juan Velasco Alvarado on December 19, 1973, in Lima. *Prensa Latina* (Lima), December 20, 1973.

equipment. In September 1972, a ten-year Soviet-Peruvian fisheries cooperation agreement was signed, which included a survey of Peru's offshore waters and fishery resources.

The overthrow of the Allende government in September 1973 focused Moscow's attention on Peru as the most promising member of the "anticapitalist" and "anti-imperialist" front in South America. At the end of 1973, Peru became the first country in the Western Hemisphere, except for Cuba, to receive Soviet military assistance. Moscow and Lima had been discussing the subject for nearly two years. But it was reportedly only after the fall of Allende that the Soviet Union agreed to provide an estimated 200 T-55 medium tanks, heavy artillery, and other equipment to the Peruvian Army on extremely generous, concessionary terms. [87] Delivery of the tanks began in November 1973; and shortly thereafter, 15 Soviet military advisors arrived in Lima to provide instruction in the use of the equipment. [88] It was not until the end of December 1973, after it was reported in the Western press, that the Velasco government admitted the arrival of the Soviet arms while still denying the presence of Soviet military advisors. [89]

Soviet military assistance was alleged to be another example of the Velasco government's capacity to make "independent decisions" [90] (that is, to take anti-American measures), but it also had domestic and regional repercussions that may prove to be far-reaching. In Peru, it strengthened the uneasiness of certain military and civilian sectors concerning President Velasco's policy of close collaboration with the Soviet Union and Cuba. The armed forces are divided on this issue. Some high military officials see the risks rather than the advantages involved in the Soviet-Cuban presence. Soviet-Cuban revolutionary activism in Chile under the Allende regime is still fresh in their minds. They are far from convinced, as President Velasco claims to be, that the USSR is a

[87] *Washington Star-News*, February 1974, and Western intelligence sources.
[88] *Ibid.*
[89] *Latin* (Buenos Aires), December 19, 1973.
[90] See President Velasco's statement on December 19, 1973, reported by *Latin* on same date.

benign and friendly country that has suffered from unfair propaganda.

The military aid agreement also signaled another step forward in Peru's ambitious and costly weapons acquisition program, which totalled $1 billion during the first five years (1969-73) of the Velasco government.[91] Peru's efforts to shift the military balance in the Andean region is causing great concern in Ecuador, Bolivia, and Chile (which has lost its former position of arms superiority), and has contributed to an expanded military modernization program in these countries. Chile in particular fears a revanchist attempt by the Peruvian military to retake land lost to Chile during the War of the Pacific (1879-83). Now that Peru has achieved superiority in numbers and quality of weapons and warships, it favors a ten-year arms freeze in Latin America to solidify its position in the Andean region.

The potential importance of the Peruvian revolution was not lost on the Soviet leaders. Moscow realized that the Velasco regime, by preparing the road to Socialist development and pursuing a foreign policy with strong anti-American overtones, could help to weaken American influence in Latin America. Peru is viewed by Moscow as a harbinger of a powerful anti-imperialist and anticapitalist trend within the Latin American military. Ambitious generals in Bolivia, Ecuador, and Panama have already been influenced by the Peruvian model. In varying degrees, they have committed themselves to domestic social reforms, an expansion of the state sector, restriction of foreign investment, and income redistribution benefiting the impoverished masses. Moscow perceives that radical nationalist regimes of the Peruvian type, which view anti-Americanism as a source of cohesion and bargaining strength, are much more susceptible to Soviet influence through normal diplomatic and economic channels, and more vulnerable to long-term Communist infiltration than to futile efforts to subvert them directly.

[91] *World Military Expenditure, 1971* (Washington: US Arms Control and Disarmament Agency, 1972); and *The Military Balance, 1971/72 and 1972/73* (London: International Institute for Strategic Studies, 1972 and 1973).

Despite its heightened interest in the Peruvian revolution, Moscow seems to be following the kind of policy of limited economic commitment and political risk that was evident in its policy *vis-à-vis* Chile. General Velasco is considered by the Soviet leaders to be a not altogether reliable "friend and ally" who is equally capable of switching to close cooperation with the United States or of increasing his anti-Americanism. Much depends on the subtlety of Washington's policy and the balance of political forces within the Peruvian military-technical elite and Peruvian society.

Peru's military leaders are not likely soon to abandon their ambitions to become a major influence within the Third World, and to forge an effective alliance of Third World mineral exporting countries capable of dictating terms to the industrial world. As long as Peru's radical domestic reforms and *realpolitik* overseas seem to be yielding dividends, US-Peruvian relations are more likely to be characterized by conflict and coolness. In any event, Moscow's relations with Peru consistently reflect its strategy of lending conditional support and encouragement to whatever actions weaken the American position in the Western Hemisphere.

10

Balance Sheet of Soviet Progress

In Latin America, the Soviet Union finds a rapidly changing environment that it seeks to exploit and influence for its own advantage. The Soviet position in Latin America is no doubt stronger today than it was a decade ago, but it still is very far from a commanding position. The Russians have established a major presence only in Cuba, where their relations have colonial overtones. In the rest of Latin America, the United States, the West European countries, and Japan have the strongest influence on the course of events. This situation is unlikely to change in the foreseeable future. Soviet progress has been gradual and not without setbacks; but it has gained a certain momentum, in contrast to the American policy of strategic retrenchment and a low profile in the region.

Soviet influence has grown not because of the spread of Communist ideology, although Marxist ideas are widespread and influential, but as a result of efforts made on different levels to make friends—especially economic aid and political support of the Latin American countries in their disputes with the United States. Soviet policy always stresses that this assistance, in contrast with imperialist aid, is "selfless" and free of political strings; neither military bases nor political conformity are expected in return. Nevertheless, Soviet economic support is given with an eye to dislodging the United States and Western countries from raw materials and energy sources, strengthening the state sector of the economy, and creating a friendly, Soviet-trained military and technical elite that favors the noncapitalist path of development. In pursuit of its aims, Moscow has not hesitated to cooperate with military dictatorships and reactionary regimes as well as with ultraleftist revolutionaries.

The only striking Soviet gain in Latin America so far—Cuba—was not achieved by "correct" Marxist-Leninist analysis or by the triumph of "united front" tactics. The Soviet Union became entrenched by invitation. Russia's acquisition of a client state in the Caribbean was the outcome of a radical nationalist revolution and Fidel Castro's hatred of the United States, not outside pressure. Moreover, Cuba has proved to be a not unmixed blessing to the Soviet Union. A great deal of money and effort have been invested, but the loans and arms have not always been used in ways that Moscow approved. Soviet help was provided to make Cuba a showcase for the superiority of socialism, but its meager economic performance has been surpassed by most other Latin American countries, with the notable exceptions of Haiti and Uruguay. Its achievements in the fields of health and education were more impressive; but even here, the Castro regime has admitted in recent years the persistence of severe problems in the quality of educational and health services provided.

Soviet policy aims at extending its influence without provoking a head-on clash with the United States and adversely affecting the far from smooth course of detente. Allende's Chile and Velasco's Peru received some Soviet support but nothing like the massive economic assistance provided to Cuba. Moscow's reluctance to come to the rescue of the Allende government was a deep disappointment and a blow to Moscow's prestige in Latin America. After the fall of Allende, Peru replaced Chile in the Soviet scheme as the leader of the anti-American front in South America and became Cuba's closest ally in Latin America and the Third World.[92]

What directions Soviet policy is likely to take in the years to come, and how the Latin American countries are likely to react, are by no means clear. Most likely, Moscow will continue to seize opportunities to turn anti-American nationalism in Latin America to its own advantage, and to erode the American position in the Hemisphere. But the lack of deeply established Soviet interests in the area (aside from Cuba), its remoteness from the Soviet Union and proximity to the United States, and Moscow's stake in detente tend to reduce the prospects of a more aggressive policy. On the other hand, Soviet ideology and interests require a commitment to "progressive" social change. Worldwide rivalry with both the United States and China also prompts Russia to seek political gains in Third World areas like Latin America that are otherwise of no vital importance. Despite detente, Moscow shows no signs of abandoning its policy of taking advantage of any change in Latin America that can be used against the United States.

During the 1960s, Moscow and Washington had an understanding concerning spheres of influence, and certain rules of the game are still observed. But strategic parity, America's strategic withdrawal from exposed overseas positions, its growing dependence on foreign raw materials and energy supplies, and the halting progress of East-West detente are reopening many questions. The growth of Russia's overseas military and economic capabilities, its expanding presence in Latin America, and its willingness to exploit American weaknesses and conflicts in the region are likely to affect the rules of the game, at least in the longer run. There is now a far greater acceptance of interpenetration of what used to be considered traditional "spheres of influence," and Latin America has ceased to be considered an exclusively American preserve, even by Washington.

[92]Peruvian-Cuban relations became perceptibly closer in 1972 and 1973. Peru's Foreign Minister visited Cuba in October 1973, and signed a joint declaration reaffirming their efforts to create a new Latin American organization from which the US would be excluded. See *Granma* (English edition), November 11, 1973, for text of the communique.

Moscow is banking on strategic parity (a better "correlation of world forces") and East-West detente to create a political climate in Latin America that favors the radicalization of its politics, disintegration of the inter-American system, greater independence from the United States, the elimination of American ownership of strategic raw materials and energy reserves, and closer ties with the Soviet Union and the Socialist camp generally. Political support and economic aid will continue to be employed in an effort to strengthen this process, even though the results, measured in terms of political influence, are often meager.

Latin America's place in East-West detente has never been clarified. The region has never had decisive geographic importance in world politics, and even the Panama Canal has lost much of its strategic value in the nuclear era. Access to military facilities in the Caribbean and South America may be useful, but are by no means vital to the security of either Moscow or Washington. To a considerable extent, the future of the region depends on America's capabilities and policies, which are less clear than Soviet aims. Much hinges on the general trend of American policy between the extremes of global activism and isolationism, and on the decision as to how high Latin America ranks in America's global priorities and commitments. The further growth of American isolationism could open up new possibilities for the Soviet Union, particularly if the Latin American countries came to believe that more can be gained by confrontation than by cooperation with the United States. The weakening of the American position could ultimately lead to the dismantling of the inter-American system and the neutralization of Latin America. Further American retreat seems unlikely at present, especially in view of Secretary of State Henry Kissinger's initiatives (called the "New Dialogue") since the end of 1973 to strengthen inter-American solidarity and resolve outstanding disputes and conflicts. But the possibility cannot be altogether dismissed.

On the Soviet side, the expansion of diplomatic and economic aid activities in the 1970s might also lead to a progressive adjustment of the foreign policies of some of the Latin American states to this "new reality," especially if accompanied by a Soviet military presence. It should be remembered that the image of rising Axis military and economic power in the 1930s facilitated the spread of Fascist ideology and pro-Fascist regimes in the Hemisphere. In some cases, such as the "Integralistas" in Brazil, there was an ideological affinity: in others, such as in Chile and Argentina, advocates of neutrality were impressed by the growing power of Hitler's Germany and Mussolini's Italy, and urged their countries not to become involved in the coming European war. Outright pro-Axis policies were adopted in some instances; in others, "neutral" or nonantagonistic postures were assumed. Something like this might happen again, but it is important not to exaggerate the probable extent of this shift in view of the many external powers now vying for political influence and economic advantage in the region.

In any event, Latin America is now exposed to a multiplicity of influences from outside the Hemisphere. In their quest for greater freedom of maneuver, there is a good chance that self-interest and the instinct of survival will lead most, though perhaps not all, of these countries to resist domination by either of the superpowers. The Latin American countries have entered the world arena and are asserting their claim to participate in those decisions that affect their destiny. The time is past when Latin America could be analyzed in isolation from the process of East-West detente, the emerging great power equilibrium, and the major problems of world growth and stability.

APPENDIX

Status of Latin American Communist and Ultraleftist Parties

1973

Country	Name of Party	Estimated Membership	Position	Legal
Argentina	Communist Party of Argentina	70,000	Pro-Moscow	Yes
	People's Revolutionary Army (ERP)	Not known	Trotskyite	No
	Armed Forces of Liberation (FAL)	Not known	Pro-Castro	No
	Revolutionary Armed Forces (FAR)	Not known	Pro-Castro	No
	Montoneros	Not known	Castroite-Peronist	Yes
	Fuerzas Armadas Peronistas (FAP)	Not known	Castroite-Peronist	Yes
Barbados	No Communist Party			
	People's Progressive Movement (PPM)	Negligible	Far Left	Yes
Bolivia	Communist Party of Bolivia (PCB/S)	1,500	Pro-Moscow	No
	Communist Party of Bolivia (PCB/C)	1,100	Pro-Peking	No
	Revolutionary Workers Party	175	Trotskyite	No
	Army of National Liberation (ELN)	Not known	Pro-Castro	No
Brazil	Communist Party of Brazil (PCB)	7,000	Pro-Moscow	No
	Communist Party of Brazil (CPB)	Not known	Pro-Peking	No
	National Liberation Action (ALN)	Negligible	Pro-Castro	No
	Popular Revolutionary Vanguard (VPR)	Not known	Pro-Castro	no

Country	Name of Party	Estimated Membership	Position	Legal
Chile	Communist Party of Chile	12,000	Pro-Moscow	No
	Leftist Revolutionary Movement (MIR)	Negligible	Pro-Castro	No
	Popular Workers Vanguard	Negligible	Undetermined	No
Colombia	Communist Party of Colombia (PCC)	10,000	Pro-Moscow	Yes
	Communist Party of Colombia Marxist-Leninist (PCC/ML)	1,000	Pro-Peking	Yes
	Colombian Revolutionary Armed Forces (FARC)	100[b]	Guerrilla Arm of the PCC	No
	Army of National Liberation (ELN)	100[b]	Pro-Castro	No
	Popular Army of Liberation	50[b]	Pro-Peking	No
Costa Rica	Popular Vanguard Party (PVN)	1,000	Pro-Moscow Communist Party	No
Cuba	Cuban Communist Party (PCC)	125,000	Independent[a]	Yes
Dominican Republic	Dominican Popular Movement (MPD)	385	Pro-Castro	No
	Dominican Communist Party (PCD)	470	Pro-Moscow	No
	14th of June Revolutionary Movement (MR 1J4)	300	Splintered- various ideologies	No
	Communist Party of Dominican Republic (PCRD)	145	Maoist	No
	Proletarian Voice (VP)	65	Pro-Peking	No
	Popular Socialist Party (PSP)	40	Pro-Moscow	No

Country	Name of Party	Estimated Membership	Position	Legal
Ecuador	Communist Party of Ecuador (PLE)	500	Pro-Moscow	Yes
	Communist Party of Ecuador Marxist-Leninist (PCE/ML)	250	Pro-Peking	Yes
	Revolutionary Social Party of Ecuador	450	Undetermined	Yes
El Salvador	Communist Party of El Salvador (PCES)	125	Pro-Moscow (with violent action faction)	No
Guadeloupe	Communist Party of Guadeloupe	3,000	Pro-Moscow	Yes
Guatemala	Guatemalan Labor Party (PGT)	750	Pro-Moscow (with small terrorist force known as the revolutionary Armed Forces or PGT/FAR)	No
Guyana	Working People's Vanguard Party (WPVP)	100	Pro-Moscow	Yes
	People's Progressive Party (PPP)	100c	Pro-Moscow	Yes
Haiti	Unified Party of Haitian Communists (PUCH)	Not known	PUCH resulted from the merger in 1968 of Pro-Moscow and Pro-Havana line parties and is inactive	No

Country	Name of Party	Estimated Membership	Position	Legal
Honduras	Communist Party of Honduras (PCH)	300	Pro-Moscow (with revolutionary wing)	No
Jamaica	No Communist Party			
Martinique	Communist Party of Martinique	1,000	Pro-Moscow	Yes
Mexico	Mexican Communist Party (PCM)	5,000	Independent	Yes
	Socialist People's Party (PPS)	10,000	Pro-Moscow	Yes
Nicaragua	Socialist Party of Nicaragua (PSN)	60	Pro-Moscow	No
	Communist Party of Nicaragua[d]	40	Pro-Moscow	No
	Sandinista National Liberation Front (FSLN)	50	Pro-Castro guerrilla group	No
Panama	People's Democratic Party (PDP)	500	Pro-Moscow	No
	Castroite Movement of Revolutionary Unity (MUR)	50	Pro-Castro	No
Paraguay	Communist Party of Paraguay	3,500	Mainly pro-Moscow	No

Country	Name of Party	Estimated Membership	Position	Legal
Peru	Communist Party of Peru (PCP/S)	3,200	Pro-Moscow	Yes
	Communist Party of Peru (PCP/C)	1,200	Pro-Peking	Yes
	Movement of the Revolutionary Left (MIR)	Not known	Pro-Castro	Yes
	Army of National Liberation (ELN)	Not known	Pro-Castro	Yes
Trinidad and Tobago	No Communist Party			
Uruguay	Uruguayan Communist Party (PCU)	22,000	Pro-Moscow	No
	National Liberation Movement (MLN) (Tupamaros)	800-1,000	Independent	No
Venezuela	Communist Party of Venezuela (PCV)	8,000	Pro-Moscow	Yes
	Movement to Socialism (MAS)	4,500	Independent	Yes
	Union for Advancement (UA)	Not known[e]	Communist Front	Yes

[a]Less independent and more pro-Soviet than at any time since the Cuban revolution.

[b]Unofficial estimates.

[c]The PPP is dominated by approximately 100 hard-core Communists, but has a substantial electoral following.

[d]Formerly Nicaraguan Socialist Workers Party, but name was changed in 1971.

[e]During the December 1968 election, the UA obtained 103,368 votes.

Source: US Department of State, Bureau of Intelligence and Research, *World Strength of the Communist Party Organizations* (Washington: US Government Printing Office, 1973).

SELECTED BIBLIOGRAPHY

Books

Abel, Elie. *The Missile Crisis* (New York: Lippincott, 1966).

Aguilar, Luis E. *Marxism in Latin America* (New York: Knopf, 1968).

Cable, James. *Gunboat Diplomacy* (London: Chatto and Windus, 1971).

Carlton, Robert G. *Soviet Image of Contemporary Latin America, A Documentary History, 1960-68* (Austin: University of Texas Press, 1970).

Clissold, Stephen, ed. *Soviet Relations with Latin America, 1918-1968, A Documentary Survey* (New York: Oxford University Press, 1970).

Crasweller, Robert. *The Caribbean Community, Changing Societies and U.S. Policy* (New York: Praeger, 1972).

de Kadt, Emanuel. *Patterns of Foreign Influence in the Caribbean* (London: Oxford University Press, 1972).

Duncan, W.R. *Soviet Policy in Developing Countries* (Waltham, Mass.: Ginn-Blaisdell, 1970).

Goldman, Marshall I. *Soviet Foreign Aid* (New York: Praeger, 1967).

Gonzalez, Edward. *Cuba Under Castro, The Limits of Charisma* (Boston: Houghton Mifflin, 1974).

Gott, Richard. *Guerrilla Movements in Latin America* (Garden City: Doubleday, 1971).

Jackson, D. Bruce. *Castro, the Kremlin, and Communism in Latin America* (Baltimore: Johns Hopkins University Press, 1969).

Joshua, Wynfred, and Gibert, Stephen P. *Arms for the Third World, Soviet Military Aid Diplomacy* (Baltimore: Johns Hopkins University Press, 1969).

Karol, K.S. *Guerrillas in Power, The Course of the Cuban Revolution* (New York: Hill and Wang, 1970).

Moss, Robert. *Urban Guerrillas* (London: Temple Smith, 1972).

Muller, Kurt. *Foreign Aid Program of the Soviet Bloc* (New York: Walker, 1967).

Oswald, J. Gregory and Strover, Anthony J., eds. *The Soviet Union and Latin America* (New York: Praeger, 1968).

Plank, John, ed. *Cuba and the United States* (Washington: Brookings Institution, 1967).

Poppino, Rollie, *International Communism in Latin America, A History of the Movement, 1917-1963* (New York: Free Press, 1964).

Ransom, Harry H. *The Communist Tide in Latin America* (Austin: University of Texas Press, 1972).

Suarez, Andres. *Cuba, Castroism and Communism, 1959-1966* (Cambridge: MIT Press, 1967).

Suchlicki, Jaime. *Cuba in Revolution* (New York: Doubleday, 1972).

Szulc, Tad, ed. *The United States and the Caribbean* (Englewood Cliffs, N.J.: Prentice-Hall, 1971).

Theberge, James D. *Soviet Seapower in the Caribbean, Political and Strategic Implications* (New York: Praeger, 1972).

_____. *Russia in the Caribbean* (Parts I and II (Washington: Center for Strategic and International Studies, Georgetown University, 1973).

Thomas, Hugh. *Cuba, The Pursuit of Freedom* (New York: Harper and Row, 1971).

Articles, Papers, and Reports

Crassweller, Robert D. *Cuba and the U.S.* Foreign Policy Association Report No. 207 (October 1971).

Dinerstein, Herbert. "Soviet Policy in Latin America," *American Political Science Review,* vol. 61 (March 1967).

Pizinger, Donald D. "Present Soviet Policy in Latin America," *Naval War College Review,* vol. 21, no. 8 (April 1969).

Quester, G.H. "Missiles in Cuba, 1970," *Foreign Affairs,* vol. 49, no. 3 (April 1971).

Roberts, Jack L. "The Growing Soviet Naval Presence in the Caribbean: Its Politico-Military Impact Upon the United States," *Naval War College Review,* vol. 23, no. 10 (June 1971).

Theberge, J.D. "Soviet Navy in the Caribbean: The Doorstep Challenge," *Navy — The Magazine of Sea Power* (March 1971).

_____. "Soviet Naval Power: Political and Strategic Considerations," in Robert Moss, ed., *The Stability of the Caribbean* (London and Washington: Institute for the Study of Conflict and Center for Strategic and International Studies, 1973).

Treadwell, T.K. "Soviet Oceanography Today," *U.S. Naval Institute Proceedings,* vol. 93 (March 1965).

Wilson, Desmond P., Jr. "Soviet-Cuban Relations," *Orbis,* vol. 12, no. 2 (Summer 1968).

Congressional Publications

Communist Threat to the United States Through the Caribbean. Hearings before the Subcommittee to Investigate the Administration of the Internal Security Act and Other Internal Security Laws of the Committee on the Judiciary, US Senate, 90th Congress, First Session, Part 18, June 28, 1967, on Soviet and Cuban Fishermen (Washington: US Government Printing Office, 1967).

Communist Threat to the United States Through the Caribbean. Hearings before the Subcommittee to Investigate the Administration of the Internal Security Act and Other Internal Security Laws of the Committee on the Judiciary, US Senate, 91st Congress, Second Session, Part 21, June 30, 1970, on Coast Guard policy and operations with respect to foreign vessel activities in or near US waters off the state of Florida (Washington: US Government Printing Office, 1970).

Communist Threat to the United States Through the Caribbean. Hearings before the Subcommittee to Investigate the Administration of the Innernal Security Act and Other Internal Security Laws of the Committee on the Judiciary, US Senate, 92nd Congress, First Session, Part 23, February 25, 1971, Testimony of Francisco Antonio Tiera Alfonso (Washington: US Government Printing Office, 1971).

Cuba and the Caribbean. Hearings before the Subcommittee on Inter-American Affairs of the Committee on Foreign Affairs, House of Representatives, 91st Congress, Second Session, July 8-August 3, 1970 (Washington: US Government Printing Office, 1970).

Cuba and the Caribbean. Hearings before the Subcommittee on Inter-American Affairs of the Committee on Foreign Affairs, House of Representatives, 91st Congress, Second Session, July 8, 9, 10, 13, 20, 27, 31 and August 3, 1970 (Washington: US Government Printing Office, 1970).

Soviet Naval Activities in Cuba. Hearings before the Subcommittee on Inter-American Affairs of the Committee on Foreign Affairs, House of Representatives, 91st Congress, Second Session, September 30, October 13, November 19 and 24, 1970 (Washington: US Government Printing Office, 1971).

Soviet Naval Activities in Cuba. Hearings before the Subcommittee on Inter-American Affairs of the Committee on Foreign Affairs, House of Representatives, 92nd Congress, First Session, September 28, 1971 (Washington: US Government Printing Office, 1971).

Soviet Policy in the Caribbean. Statement by James D. Theberge before the Committee on Internal Security, House of Representatives, October 21, 1971, and published in the report of the Committee Hearings entitled *The Theory and Practice of Communism in 1971: Latin America* (Washington: US Government Printing Office, 1972).

Survey of the Alliance for Progress. A study prepared at the request of the Subcommittee on American Republic Affairs of the Committee on Foreign Relations, US Senate, 90th Congress, Second Session, January 15, 1968 (Washington: US Government Printing Office, 1968).

United States Policy Towards Cuba. Hearings before the Committee on Foreign Relations, US Senate, 92nd Congress, First Session, September 16, 1971. On S. J. resolutions 146, 148 and 160 (Washington: US Government Printing Office, 1971).

National Strategy Information Center, Inc.

Strategy Papers

Edited by Frank N. Trager and William Henderson
With the assistance of Dorothy E. Nicolosi

The Soviet Presence in Latin America by James D. Theberge, June 1974

The Horn of Africa by J. Bowyer Bell, Jr., December 1973

Research and Development and the Prospects for International Security by Frederick Seitz and Rodney W. Nichols, December 1973

Raw Material Supply in a Multipolar World by Yuan-li Wu, October 1973

The People's Liberation Army: Communist China's Armed Forces by Angus M. Fraser, August 1973

Nuclear Weapons and the Atlantic Alliance by Wynfred Joshua, May 1973

How to Think About Arms Control and Disarmament by James E. Dougherty, May 1973

The Military Indoctrination of Soviet Youth by Leon Goure, January 1973

The Asian Alliance: Japan and United States Policy by Franz Michael and Gaston J. Sigur, October 1972

Iran, The Arabian Peninsula, and the Indian Ocean by R. M. Burrell and Alvin J. Cottrell, September 1972

Soviet Naval Power: Challenge for the 1970s by Norman Polmar, April 1972 (Out of print)

How Can We Negotiate with the Communists? by Gerald L. Steibel, March 1972

Soviet Political Warfare Techniques, Espionage and Propaganda in the 1970s by Lyman B. Kirkpatrick, Jr., and Howland H. Sargeant, January 1972

The Soviet Presence in the Eastern Mediterranean by Lawrence L. Whetten, September 1971

The Military Un*balance*
Is the U.S. Becoming a Second-Class Power? June 1971

The Future of South Vietnam by Brigadier F. P. Serong, February 1971 (Out of print)

Strategy and National Interests: Reflections for the Future by Bernard Brodie, January 1971

The Mekong River: A Challenge in Peaceful Development for Southeast Asia by Eugene R. Black, December 1970

Problems of Strategy in the Pacific and Indian Oceans by George G. Thomson, October 1970

Soviet Penetration into the Middle East by Wynfred Joshua, July 1970. Revised edition, October 1971

Australian Security Policies and Problems by Justus M. van der Kroef, May 1970

Detente: Dilemma or Disaster? by Gerald L. Steibel, July 1969

The Prudent Case for Safeguard by William R. Kintner, June
1969

Forthcoming

Soviet Naval Power: Challenge for the 1970s, revised edition,
by Norman Polmar

The Middle East: New Opportunities for the Kremlin by R. M.
Burrell

The Development of Strategic Weapons by Norman Polmar

Contemporary Soviet Defense Policy by Benjamin S. Lambeth